WHY READ AND STUDY THE WORDS OF THE HEBREW PROPHETS?

In the 1960s Simon and Garfunkel famously sang that "the words of the prophets are written on the subway walls and tenement halls." They meant that what a society often needs to hear most is spoken by people who are marginalized and excluded and denied a voice, so they create communication channels of their own. This was just as true of the ancient nation of Israel as it was of the New York City those two singers knew. God had chosen to work through the people of Israel to model his love and justice for every nation. But their society had become corrupt, exploitive, and immoral. So God sent them a message, again and again, through unlikely figures who mostly came from outside the structures of power and privilege. They were the Hebrew prophets.

These messengers got the nation's attention by creating memorable poems and songs that were replete with vivid imagery and striking word plays. Through them they cried out against injustice and called the people back to God's purposes. Unfortunately the people didn't respond and as a divine judgment they were conquered and carried off into exile. But the very rejection of the prophets' message caused them to create written collections of the words to their poems and songs. These were passed down through the centuries and became part of the Bible, where we can still read them today. When we do, we find that they speak a message about love and justice that we need to hear and heed just as urgently as the people it was originally spoken to.

If you choose to read the words of these graffiti artists of the eighth and seventh centuries BC, you won't have a comfortable experience. You'll be challenged to make changes in your life and to work for changes in your society. You'll begin to see life from an incisive divine perspective that will change your view of the world and your place in it forever. And all of this will come through an encounter with some of the most powerful and moving poetry ever written. So get those friends of yours who want to make this a better world—you know who they are—and read and discuss the words of the prophets with them.

This guide will get you started by introducing you to a group of prophets whose collected works are all relatively short and who lived before the Babylonian exile. For these reasons, they're called the pre-exilic minor prophets.

UNDERSTANDING THE
BOOKS OF THE BIBLE

PROPHETS
BEFORE
THE EXILE

Also available in the
UNDERSTANDING THE BOOKS OF THE BIBLE series:

PROPHETS BEFORE THE EXILE

AMOS
HOSEA
MICAH
ZEPHANIAH
NAHUM
HABAKKUK

Christopher R. Smith

IVP Connect

An imprint of InterVarsity Press
Downers Grove, Illinois

InterVarsity Press
P.O. Box 1400, Downers Grove, IL 60515-1426
World Wide Web: www.ivpress.com
E-mail: email@ivpress.com

InterVarsity Press® is the book-publishing division of InterVarsity Christian Fellowship/USA®, a movement of students and faculty active on campus at hundreds of universities, colleges and schools of nursing in the United States of America, and a member movement of the International Fellowship of Evangelical Students. For information about local and regional activities, write Public Relations Dept., InterVarsity Christian Fellowship/USA, 6400 Schroeder Rd., P.O. Box 7895, Madison, WI 53707-7895, or visit the IVCF website at <www.intervarsity.org>.

All Scripture quotations, unless otherwise indicated, are taken from THE HOLY BIBLE, NEW INTERNATIONAL VERSION®, NIV® *Copyright © 1973, 1978, 1984, 2011 by Biblica, Inc.™ Used by permission. All rights reserved worldwide.*

Design: Cindy Kiple
Images: © Stella Levi/iStockphoto

ISBN 978-0-8308-5814-9

Printed in the United States of America ∞

P	20	19	18	17	16	15	14	13	12	11	10	9	8	7	6	5	4	3	2	1
Y	30	29	28	27	26	25	24	23	22	21	20	19	18	17	16	15	14	13			

CONTENTS

HOW THESE STUDY GUIDES ARE DIFFERENT

Did you know you could read and study the Bible without using any chapters or verses? The books of the Bible are real "books." They're meant to be experienced the same way other books are: as exciting, interesting works that keep you turning pages right to the end and then make you want to go back and savor each part. The UNDERSTANDING THE BOOKS OF THE BIBLE series of study guides will help you do that with the Bible.

While you can use these guides with any version or translation, they're especially designed to be used with *The Books of the Bible*, an edition of the Scriptures from Biblica that takes out the chapter and verse numbers and presents the biblical books in their natural form. Here's what people are saying about reading the Bible this way:

> I love it. I find myself understanding Scripture in a new way, with a fresh lens, and I feel spiritually refreshed as a result. I learn much more through stories being told and, with this new format, I feel the truth of the story come alive for me.

> Reading Scripture this way flows beautifully. I don't miss the chapter and verse numbers. I like them gone. They got in the way.

> I've been a reader of the Bible all of my life. But after reading just a few pages without chapters and verses, I was amazed at what I'd been missing all these years.

You can find out more about *The Books of the Bible* and get a low-cost copy by visiting www.biblica.com/thebooks or by calling (800) 524-1588. Watch the site for a four-volume set comprising the entire Bible, now in progress. Trade editions from Zondervan are available online or through your favorite Christian book retailer.

For people who are used to chapters and verses, reading and studying the Bible without them may take a little getting used to. It's like when you get a new smartphone, or a new computer or tablet. You have to unlearn some old ways of doing things and learn some new ways. But it's not too long until you catch on to how the new system works and you find you can do a lot of things you couldn't do before.

Here are some of the ways you and your group will have a better experience of the Scriptures by using these study guides.

YOU'LL FOLLOW THE NATURAL FLOW OF BIBLICAL BOOKS

This guide will take you through the collected oracles of the prophets who spoke to Israel and Judah before the Babylonian exile. You won't go chapter-by-chapter through these books, because the chapter divisions in the Bible often come at the wrong places and break up the flow of individual compositions. Did you know that the chapter divisions used in most modern Bibles were added more than a thousand years after the biblical books were written? And that the verse numbers were added more than three centuries after that? If you grew up with the chapter-and-verse system, it may feel like part of the inspired Word of God. But it's not. Those little numbers aren't holy, and when you read and study the words of the prophets without them, you'll hear their message more clearly than ever before.

YOU'LL UNDERSTAND WHOLE BOOKS

Imagine going to a friend's house to watch a movie you've never seen before. After only a couple of scenes, your friend stops the film and says, "So, tell me what you think of it so far." When you give your best shot at a reply, based on the little you've seen, your friend says, "You know, there's a scene in another movie that always makes me think of this one." He switches to a different movie and before you know it, you're watching a scene from the middle of another film.

Who would ever try to watch a movie this way? Yet many study guides take this approach to the Bible. They have you read a few paragraphs from one book, then jump to a passage in another book. The UNDERSTANDING THE BOOKS OF THE BIBLE series doesn't do that. Instead, these study guides focus on understanding the message and meaning of one book at a time. Your group will read through these six collections of prophetic oracles in their entirety, not just selected chapters or verses.

Sessions 1, 6, 12, 16, 18, and 20 are overviews that will let you experience each of the collections as a whole, to prepare you for considering their individual oracles. Reading through an entire book at once will be like viewing a whole movie before zooming in on one scene. Groups that read books of the Bible aloud together have a great experience doing this. (If you've never done it before, give it a try—you'll be surprised at how well it flows and how fast the time passes.)

Reading each book aloud together in your group is the recommended approach, but you can also listen to a professional recording. If you do, you should listen to these books in the latest update to the New International Version (NIV), since that's the translation used in *The Books of the Bible* and in these studies. You can listen online to the prophetic books at biblica.com/bibles/audio/niv. For these overview sessions, the discussion will be briefer and designed to allow people to share their overall impressions.

It will be helpful for group members to read the introduction to The Prophets in *The Books of the Bible* before starting this study guide, and the introductions to each of the books before you read them aloud together. (If you're using a different edition, these introductions are also available separately from InterVarsity Press in the book *Read the Bible Smarter, Not Harder*, ISBN 978-1-60657-045-6.)

Group leaders should take a moment after each of these readings to allow people to ask about any words or phrases they didn't understand and to let the group work to understand them together.

YOU'LL DECIDE FOR YOURSELVES WHAT TO DISCUSS

In each session of this study guide there are many options for discussion. While each session could be completed by a group in about an hour and a half, any one of the questions could lead to an involved conversation. There's no need to cut the conversation short to try to "get through it all." Group leaders should read through all the questions ahead of time and decide which one(s) to begin with, and what order to take them up in. If you do get into an involved discussion of one question, you can leave out some of the others, or you can extend the study over more than one meeting if you do want to cover all of them.

TOGETHER, YOU'LL SPEAK AND HEAR THE WORD OF GOD

Each session gives creative suggestions for reading the oracles you'll be discussing in a way that brings out their natural structure and emphases. You'll have the best experience with this guide by using *The Books of the Bible*, because the natural sections it marks off by white space match up with the individual oracles you'll be discussing. Nevertheless, if you're using another edition of the Bible, you'll still be able to identify these sections easily because they'll be indicated by their opening lines or by some other means that makes them obvious.

EVERYBODY WILL PARTICIPATE

There's plenty of opportunity for everyone in the group to participate. Everyone can take turns reading the oracles that you'll be considering. Group members can also read the session introduction aloud, or the discussion questions. As a leader, you can easily involve quiet people by giving them these opportunities. And everyone will feel that they can speak up and answer the questions, because they're not looking for "right answers." Instead, they invite the group to work together to understand the Bible.

YOU'LL ALL SHARE DEEPLY

The discussion questions will invite you to share deeply about your ideas and experiences. The answers to these questions can't be found just by "looking them up." They require reflection on the meaning of each oracle, in the wider context of the collection it belongs to, in light of your personal experience. These aren't the kinds of abstract, academic questions that make the discussion feel like a test. Instead, they'll connect the Bible passage to your life in practical, personal, relational ways.

To create a climate of trust where this kind of deep sharing is encouraged, here are a couple of ground rules that your group should agree to at its first meeting:

- *Confidentiality.* Group members agree to keep what is shared in the group strictly confidential. "What's said in the group stays in the group."

- *Respect.* Group members will treat other members with respect at all times, even when disagreeing over ideas.

HOW TO LEAD GROUP STUDIES USING THIS GUIDE

Each session has three basic parts:

Introduction to the Study

Have a member of your group read the introduction to the session out loud to everyone. Then give group members the chance to ask questions about the introduction, and offer their own thoughts and examples.

Reading

Have people read out loud the oracles that you'll be discussing. The study guide will offer suggestions for various ways you can do this for each session. In the overview sessions, group members will take turns reading through a prophetic collection in its entirety. (In some cases, reading and discussion will be combined.)

Discussion Questions

Most questions are introduced with some observations. These may give some background to the history and culture of the ancient world, or explain where you are in an overall collection. After these observations there are suggested discussion questions. Many of them have multiple parts that are really just different ways of getting at an issue.

You don't have to discuss the questions in the order they appear in the study guide. You can choose to spend your time exploring just one or two questions, and not do the others. Or you can have shorter discussions of each question so that you do cover all of them. The group leader should read the questions and the observations that introduce them before the meeting and decide which ones to emphasize.

When you get to a given question, have someone read aloud the observations and the question. As you answer the question, interact with the observations (you can agree or disagree with them) in light of your reading from the Bible. Use only part of the question to get at the issue from one angle, or use all of the parts, as you choose.

FOR FURTHER READING AND DISCUSSION

At the end of some sessions, other passages in the prophetic book you're considering will be suggested for further reading and discussion. Your group can take some of these up if it wants to and has time. Individuals can also read and reflect on them on their own. In this way the guide will orient you to every passage in each of the books it covers.

FOR YOUR NEXT MEETING

Information will be provided at the end of certain sessions about preparations that members should make or about materials that will be needed for the next session.

TIPS FOR HOME GROUPS, SUNDAY SCHOOL CLASSES, COMMUNITY BIBLE EXPERIENCES, AND INDIVIDUAL USE

If you're using this guide in a *home group*, you may want to begin each meeting (or at least some meetings) by having dinner together. You may also want to have a time of singing and prayer before or after the study.

If you're using this guide in a *Sunday school class*, you may want to have a time of singing and prayer before or after the study.

This study guide can also be used in connection with a *community Bible experience* of the pre-exilic prophets. If you're using it in this way:

- Encourage people to read each session's Scripture passage by themselves early in the week (except for sessions 1, 6, 12, 16, 18, and 20, when the whole church should gather to hear entire collections read out loud).
- Do each session in midweek small groups.
- Invite people to write/create some response to each small-group session that could be shared in worship that weekend. These might involve poetry, journal or blog entries, artwork, dramas, videos, and so on, and especially the creative retellings that are invited in some sessions.
- During the weekend worship services, let people share these responses, and have preaching on the topic of the session that was studied that week. Speakers can gather up comments they've heard from people and draw on their own reflections to sum up the church's experience of that session. The following week will be devoted to the next session in the same way.

This guide can also be used for *individual study*. You can write out your responses to the questions in a notebook or journal. (However, we really encourage reading and studying the Bible in community!)

ISRAEL-JUDAH MAP

Locations on this map appear in **bold type** the first time they're mentioned in this study guide.

TIMELINE OF THE PROPHETS

Date BC	Prohets Active	Kings of Judah	Kings of Israel		Emperors of Assyria
800		Uzziah (792-740)	Jereboam II (782-753)	*Assyrian empire in decline*	Shalmanezer IV (782-772)
	AMOS				Assurdan III (771-754)
750		Jotham (750-735)	Zachariah (753) Shallum (752) Menahem (752-742)		Assurniari (753-746) Tiglath-pileser (745-727)
	HOSEA	Ahaz (735-715)	Pekahiah (742-740) Pekah (740-732)	*Assyrian empire resurgent*	Shalmanezer V (727-722)
	MICAH	Hezekiah (715-686)	Hoshea (732-722) *Assyrians conquer Israel*		Sargon (722-705)
700		Manasseh (697-642)			Sennacherib (705-681) *Invaded Judah*
					Esarhaddon (681-669) *Invaded Egypt*
					Ashurbanipal (669-627) *Conquered Thebes*
650		Amon (642-640)		*Assyrian empire in decline*	Sinsriskun (627-612)
	ZEPHANIAH	Josiah (640-609)			
	NAHUM HABAKKUK				*Nineveh conquered 612 BC*
600					

AMOS

EXPERIENCING THE BOOK OF
AMOS AS A WHOLE

In preparation for this session, group members should read the introductions to The Prophets and to the book of Amos in The Books of the Bible *or in* Read the Bible Smarter, Not Harder. *Give people a chance to ask any questions they have about these introductions at the start of your meeting. You can also read them in your group and discuss them before doing this session.*

INTRODUCTION

Early in the story of the Bible, God promises a man named Abraham that he'll make him and his offspring a blessing to everyone in the world. Abraham's descendants grow to become the ancient nation of Israel, and for a time that kingdom faithfully models God's purposes. But eventually it divides into two rival kingdoms, **Israel** in the north and **Judah** in the south, and both struggle to fulfill their divine destiny. Greed, idolatry, oppression, and injustice corrupt these kingdoms to the point where God has to warn them that unless they change their ways, they'll be conquered and carried off by the rising empires to the east. God's chosen messengers to deliver this warning are the prophets.

We may think of the biblical prophets as people who speak about the future, particularly the coming of Jesus as the Messiah, and we'll see later in this guide that they do this. But the bulk of their words are actually addressed to their contemporaries and are concerned with the social conditions of their time. They are prophets in another sense of the word: They speak truth to power.

While other prophets spoke to the people of Israel and Judah earlier, the first one whose words have been preserved for us in writing was named Amos. He lived in the middle of the eighth century BC in **Tekoa**, a small city south of **Jerusalem** in Judah. By his own admission, he never apprenticed with an older prophet, as some did in his day. Rather, he herded sheep and tended fig trees. This made him an unlikely candidate to become one of God's messengers. It was even more improbable when God sent Amos across the border to prophesy in the northern kingdom of Israel (although, as we'll see, he sometimes addressed Judah as well). This obscure foreigner went to the royal temple at **Bethel** and over the course of perhaps a year spoke such appalling words that Amaziah, the priest in charge, had him expelled. That ended the official part of his mission. But through the book that contains his messages, his influence continues around the world to this day.

Amos never set out to write a book. Few people in his culture could read, so a book wouldn't have been an effective means of communication. Instead, he composed short poems or songs and recited or sang them in public places. These were catchy and clever and this made them "sticky"— anyone who heard them was likely to repeat them. (Indeed, like today's advertising jingles, they were probably hard to get out of one's head.) By this means Amos's message spread far and wide. It was only when he was expelled from Israel that he or his followers felt a need to record his words, perhaps to show that he'd been faithful to the assignment God gave him, and perhaps also to show that God had warned the people and they had only themselves to blame when their corruption and oppression ended in conquest and exile.

While Amos speaks to the conditions of a particular place and time, he voices a universal concern for justice, insisting that this is the true expression of devotion to God. This makes his messages timeless and gives them as much to say to our world as to his.

READING

In this session you'll read through the whole book of Amos together. This will give you an overview that will prepare you to consider its individual sections. The reading should take fifteen to twenty minutes. You can find Amos in the Table of Contents in your Bible.

You'll see that the book is made up of about thirty short compositions. Most of them are oracles, which are poems or songs created in particular ways. They may develop an extended image, as when Amos describes the various ways the people of Israel will try to flee from their enemies. They may also use word play to bring their point home, as when Amos uses the same Hebrew term to describe how those who consider themselves the *foremost* nation, and who use the *finest* lotions, will be the *first* to go into exile. Other oracles have a repeated refrain that ties them together, as when Amos depicts various misfortunes that have struck the nation and notes after each one, "'Yet you have not returned to me,' declares the Lord."[1] An oracle can also be made up of a series of questions or statements that repeat the same basic idea.

In addition to its collection of oracles, the book of Amos also contains, near the end, a report of his expulsion from Israel and descriptions of the visions he saw that probably first prompted him to speak. All of this material is mixed rather loosely together.

Have group members take turns reading through the book out loud. Switch readers when you come to a new oracle. (This will happen often, underscoring the character of the book as a collection of brief compositions.) Don't worry if you can't identify the oracles precisely; this will be done in the following sessions. In general, a new reader should begin when Amos says something like "This is what the Lord says," "Hear this," or "This is what the Sovereign Lord showed me." If you're using *The Books of the Bible*, you can rely on the white spaces between passages to recognize where new oracles begin.

Caution: The opening series of oracles describes a number of atrocities that were committed in warfare by the nations around Israel. Have people who are willing to read difficult material take these oracles.

---

1. When Lord is written in capital letters, it stands for Yahweh, the name God used when he made a covenant or special agreement with Abraham's descendants.

If you don't understand the meaning of particular words or phrases, make a note of them. After the reading, work together as a group to understand them better.

DISCUSSION

⮑ What was it like to read a whole book of the Bible out loud in a group? How did this compare with other ways you may have read the Bible before?

⮑ What parts of the book of Amos struck you the most as you listened? What sayings did you like the best? Were there things you didn't like, that disturbed you, or that didn't make sense to you? Describe these briefly and see if the group can address some of your concerns now. Be sure to bring them up again for further discussion when you get to that part of the book in the sessions ahead.

⮑ How would you summarize Amos's overall message? (Can you do this in his own words, identifying one or more lines from the book that seem to sum up his purpose?) What are the people of Israel doing that God wants them to stop? What does God want them to do instead? Why?

⮑ Amos's longest oracles contain fewer words than the typical blog posting. His shortest oracles are brief enough to be a Facebook status update or a tweet on Twitter. Do you think a scattering of short messages like this can have a cumulative effect and be a persuasive form of communication? Why or why not?

AMOS ANNOUNCES GOD'S JUDGMENT AGAINST THE NATIONS

Book of Amos > Opening Oracles Against the Nations

INTRODUCTION

The material at the beginning of Amos is the best organized in the book. After an editor's note that introduces the prophet, identifies when he spoke, and summarizes his message, there's a series of oracles that are similar in form. They speak to the nations around Israel before addressing that kingdom as well. This series likely made up a single message that Amos delivered at a prominent location in Israel, perhaps the capital of **Samaria** but more likely the royal temple at Bethel, since Amaziah asked the king to expel him for prophesying there.

In these oracles Amos addresses the surrounding nations in order of their relationship to Israel. He begins with the unrelated Arameans and Philistines. He moves on to the Phoenicians of **Tyre**, who have made a "treaty of brotherhood" with the kingdom, and then to the Edomites, Ammonites, and Moabites, who are related to Israel through Abraham's son Isaac and nephew Lot. Finally (or so his listeners think) Amos describes God's impending judgment on the Judeans, their closest relatives and continual rivals.

With the empires of Egypt, Assyria, and Babylon in temporary decline, Israel has been asserting itself against all of these neighbors. A message that God was going to give it undisputed dominance of the region would have irresistibly attracted a crowd. The total of seven nations is just right to express God's comprehensive judgment against every nation *except* Israel—which is why Amos's words come as such a shock when he names Israel itself as an eighth target of God's impending wrath. We can picture Amos's audience cheering enthusiastically for each oracle—except the last.

READING

Have someone read the opening of the book of Amos. Then have several people take turns reading the eight oracles against the nations. (The last one ends, "'Even the bravest warriors will flee naked on that day,' declares the LORD.") Choose volunteers who are willing to read some difficult material. As you listen, you can find the locations that are mentioned on the map on page 8.

Notice how the first seven oracles follow a common pattern:

- They begin, "This is what the LORD says: 'For three sins of X, even for four, I will not relent.'" (The eighth oracle, against Israel, begins this way as well.) It's a common device of Hebrew poetry to name one number, then the next higher number, to make a definite assertion. In this case we can think of Amos telling the nations that they've got three strikes against them— no, make that four.

- Each of the first seven oracles then describes the wrongs that a nation has done. These are introduced with the word *because*. Amos names the nation at the beginning or end of the oracle and often mentions some of its prominent cities. Sometimes he uses satirical names for locations, such as the Valley of Aven (Wickedness) and Beth Eden (House of Pleasure). These highlight the corrupt, self-indulgent behavior that God is going to judge. Amos will use similar satirical names in other oracles.

- Judgment is then announced symbolically: God says he will send *fire* on the nation that will consume her *fortresses*. Fire and drought, consequences of God withholding life-giving water, are recurring images in the oracles of Amos. (The opening summary of his message contains a drought image.) Amos speaks frequently of houses of various kinds and sizes. The fortresses he mentions here are fortified houses made of stone that were royal castles and military strongholds. They were the pride of the kingdoms that built them and their destruction is a suitable symbol for the fall of those kingdoms.

• In some cases Amos then depicts the fate of a nation more literally, describing the clamor of invasion and the exile of king, nobles, and population.

DISCUSSION

1 These oracles don't argue that a nation can never go to war. But they do cry out against the atrocities that many of these kingdoms have committed either in the course of warfare or through the use of military force. All of these actions, Amos insists, are abhorrent to God, who will punish their perpetrators.

⮑ Philistines from **Gaza**, **Ashdod**, **Ashkelon**, and **Ekron** and Phoenicians from Tyre have raided neighboring countries, taken entire communities captive, and sold the people into slavery. The Edomites, who have a port on an arm of the Red Sea, are buying the captives and shipping them overseas, as brokers in an ancient international human trafficking network. What organizations do you know that are working to end human trafficking in our day? Have members of your group helped these organizations?

⮑ During a war with the Edomites, the Moabites captured their royal burial ground and burned the bones of one of their kings. This was an attempt to wipe out the heritage and culture of the nation. Where in the world today are cultural monuments and artifacts under attack? What organizations do you know that are working to protect them? Have any group members helped with this work? Do you think it's ever justifiable to destroy the evidence of certain cultural activities? Explain your answer.

◯ In a fight over **Gilead**, the Ammonites killed the unborn children of Israelite women living there. This was a particularly gruesome form of what would be called ethnic cleansing today: The Ammonites wanted to make sure that no Israelites would ever live there in the future. The Edomites may have slaughtered the women of Israel and Judah for similar reasons. (The Israelites are called the "brothers" of the Edomites because their respective ancestors, Jacob and Esau, were brothers.) Do you know anyone who has been driven out of their home or killed because of their religion or ethnicity? Why do you think so-called ethnic cleansing continues into the twenty-first century?

◯ The kingdom of **Aram** also tried to capture the region of Gilead, and its armies left the land devastated. Amos depicts them with the image of an iron threshing sled, used to separate grain from husks, leaving only chaff in its wake. If war may be permissible under some circumstances, how can armies be kept from creating wanton destruction that devastates a country?

◯ The seventh oracle is one of the places in the book where Amos speaks to his fellow Judeans. He castigates them not for atrocities in warfare but for abandoning God's laws. The ancient Israelite kingdom was intended to be a theocracy. To what extent should a modern nation seek to base its laws on religious teachings?

2 The last and longest oracle is designed to show the Israelites that many of their everyday practices are actually as wicked as the atrocities for which they believe God will judge their neighbors.

◯ Go back through this eighth oracle and identify the places where it condemns the following practices. If you can, give examples of what these practices look like in your own society.

- Exploiting human life or labor at a low price
- Denying justice to the poor
- Sexual trafficking
- Seizing assets offered as collateral for credit
- Using the proceeds of fines to maintain a lavish lifestyle
- Getting people to violate their religious convictions
- Excluding religious voices from the public arena

Which of these things would your own society be most opposed to? Which ones would it consider less serious, or even approve of? Why? What values does this reveal? How would you critique the values of your society in light of what Amos says to his?

AMOS DESCRIBES HIS MANDATE TO PROPHESY AND WARNS ISRAEL OF JUDGMENT

Book of Amos > Collected Oracles

INTRODUCTION

The book of Amos begins with an extended and well-organized oracle. After that, however, it presents shorter compositions that are more loosely grouped together. Hebrew editors and scribes considered it elegant to arrange collections of oracles by creating connections based on shared words, phrases, and images. Typically, an oracle that makes a given reference near its beginning will be placed after an oracle that makes a similar reference near its end. Amos's words have been arranged in this way, and as a result, the oracles in the book don't develop an argument sequentially and logically. Nevertheless, they do address a consistent theme: Israel is in danger of destruction if it doesn't turn from its greed, corruption, and injustice. In this session you'll begin reading and discussing the shorter oracles that make up most of the book.

READING AND DISCUSSION

1 Have someone read the next two oracles, beginning with "Hear this word, people of Israel" and ending with "The Sovereign LORD has spoken—who can but prophesy?"

The book of Amos has something of a second opening here. It presents a brief oracle in which God addresses Israel and Judah in formal language as "the whole family I brought up out of Egypt" and warns them not to let their covenant or special relationship with him make them complacent. This is a theme that will be struck several times in the rest of the book.

This second opening then introduces Amos as God's prophet and explains why he has come north to Israel. It presents an oracle in which Amos asks a series of questions that all imply the same principle: When you see one thing happening, you know something else must be going on as well. When the Israelites see the reversals and setbacks they're experiencing, they should recognize that God is beginning to punish them. Indeed, if someone like Amos is speaking to them, they should recognize that the LORD must have something in mind that he's already told his prophets about.

⊃ See if you can think of your own examples to illustrate the principle Amos develops here. (For example, "Does the check-engine light come on if there's nothing wrong with your car?")

⊃ The Israelites were blind to the dangers and opportunities of their situation because they were spiritually complacent. Look around at your own life and world. What signs can you recognize that point to impending dangers and opportunities? What attitudes and assumptions could keep you from responding to these signs?

2 Have different people read the next several oracles, beginning at these places:

- "Proclaim to the fortresses of Ashdod"
- "This is what the LORD says: 'As a shepherd rescues from the lion's mouth'"
- "Hear this and testify against the descendants of Jacob"
- "Hear this word, you cows of Bashan"
- "Go to Bethel and sin" (ending, "'boast about them, you Israelites, for this is what you love to do,' declares the Sovereign LORD")

These oracles illustrate how the materials in the book of Amos have been placed together on the basis of shared words, phrases, and images:

- The first of these oracles refers to Egypt, and the third one talks about God punishing the people for their sins; both of these things recall language found slightly earlier in the book's second opening.
- The second oracle uses the image of a lion, just like the series of questions Amos asks. (As a shepherd, Amos knows the destructive power of lions, and he employs this image evocatively; it's also in the opening summary of his message at the very start of the book.)
- The fourth of these oracles refers to Samaria, like the first and second oracles, and the fifth refers to Bethel, like the third.

These oracles also illustrate how Amos speaks from a shifting variety of perspectives to the people of Israel as he condemns their acts of oppression.

⮕ Divide your group into teams of two or three people and assign each team one or more of the oracles you've just read. Have each team determine, as best it can, what situation in the life of ancient Israel Amos is speaking to. What wrong actions or attitudes is he critiquing? How does he make his message memorable? How might you deliver the same message to your own society? After the teams have investigated their oracles, have them report back to the group as a whole.

3 Have someone read the next oracle in the book, which begins "I gave you empty stomachs in every city" and ends "prepare to meet your God." (Note how this oracle is connected to the previous one by its opening reference to bread.)

This is a slightly longer composition that consists of a series of verses that all end in the same refrain: "yet you have not returned to me." Amos describes the misfortunes the people are already experiencing and argues that these should lead them to change their ways and return to God. Instead, they're as stubborn and resistant as the Egyptians or the people of Sodom and

Gomorrah, who were destroyed by God earlier in Israel's history. (Note that Amos is now equating the "family God brought up out of Egypt" with these secular communities—there's no place for the idea that the nation's special relationship with God makes it immune from judgment.)

⮑ Many people today would consider the misfortunes Amos lists to be either natural disasters (drought, blight, mildew, locusts, epidemics) or the result of human actions (defeat in battle). But Amos describes them all as things God is doing to chastise and correct the Israelites. How would you account for this? Say which answer below you agree with most, and explain why:

a. We should still try to discern the hand of God behind natural disasters and the outcome of human conflicts today.

b. Because God had a special relationship with the ancient Israelites, he intervened directly in their affairs through the means Amos describes, in a way he doesn't do with other nations.

c. Because God had a special relationship with ancient Israel, he expected them to interpret natural disasters and the results of human conflicts in light of their relationship with him; that's what Amos is helping them do here.

d. When God spoke to the Israelites through Amos, he had to address them within the context of their worldview, in which there were no strictly "natural" events; supernatural forces were ultimately responsible for everything. The challenge for us as readers today is to appreciate how Amos was validly critiquing Israel's actions from God's perspective, even though we may understand the world differently.

FOR FURTHER READING AND DISCUSSION

• Three stanzas of a song that praises God for his power and justice have been included at various places in this collection. Amos may have written this song himself, or it may have been inspired by his words. The first stanza comes right after the last oracle you considered for this session. Make a note of its location, as you'll be invited to consider the song as a whole in session 5, once you've encountered all three stanzas in the book.

- Two very brief oracles follow, beginning "Hear this word, Israel" and "This is what the Sovereign LORD says to Israel." These are probably slogans that Amos created to shock Israel out of its complacency. What do you think the effect would have been when people heard them? What examples can you give of slogans you've heard that were similarly designed to promote social change?

INSINCERE RELIGION, LEGAL INJUSTICE, AND ECONOMIC OPPRESSION ARE RUINING ISRAEL

Book of Amos > Collected Oracles, Continued

INTRODUCTION

We saw last time how the oracles in the book of Amos are generally connected through shared words, phrases, and images. Now we'll see how some oracles that treat similar themes are actually nested inside one another. This creates an arrangement known as a *chiasm* that was considered beautiful and refined in Hebrew literature.

READING AND DISCUSSION

1 Assign four people the letters from *A* to *D* and have them read the corresponding passages identified below by their opening lines:

A Seek me and live; do not seek Bethel

A Seek the LORD and live

    B There are those who turn justice into bitterness

        C He who made the Pleiades and Orion

    B There are those who hate the one who upholds justice in court

        D You levy a straw tax on the poor

B There are those who oppress the innocent and take bribes
A Seek good, not evil, that you may live

(The last reading ends, "Perhaps the LORD God Almighty will have mercy on the remnant of Joseph." Joseph was the ancestor of Ephraim and Manasseh, the largest tribes in the kingdom of Israel, so Amos sometimes calls the kingdom by his name.)

Scholars are generally agreed that this section of the book has been assembled from three separate oracles, plus another stanza of the song you learned about last time. One oracle (reading parts A) warns the Israelites not to think they can appease God by offering worship at sacred sites like Bethel, **Gilgal**, and **Beersheba**. If the people don't do what's right and maintain justice, this worship counts for nothing. Another oracle (reading parts B) has been tucked inside this one because it addresses the related theme of "justice in the courts." The song stanza (reading part C) has been added between its first and second lines, probably because it describes God bringing "destruction on the stronghold" and the oracle about taxes warns that those who have built stone mansions will not live in them. (Note the location of this stanza as well.) Finally, an oracle (reading part D) that decries oppressive taxation has been placed between the second and third lines of the oracle about justice. The interweaving of these originally distinct compositions creates an elegant chiasm and illustrates that the reasons why the people are coming under God's judgment are interrelated: Insincere religion, legal injustice, and economic oppression are combining to corrupt the society.

⮑ Reread oracle A by itself. Have you encountered public religious observances in your culture that felt insincere to you? Why did they strike you this way? What would it look like for the participants to "seek God" rather than relying on these observances?

⮑ Reread oracle B. Amos describes the justice system being corrupted through bribes and intimidation. What measures do people use in your culture to try to get their way unfairly in court? Do you know any organizations or individuals who work on behalf of people who've been denied justice? If so, tell the group about them.

⮑ Reread oracle C. Do you believe that your country's system of taxation is generally fair? If not, how should it be changed? Do you know anyone who's working to change it as an expression of their faith in a God who cares for the poor? If so, tell their story.

⮑ Decide on something your group can do together to support one of the individuals or organizations just named.

2 Have someone read the oracle a little later in the book that begins "I hate, I despise your religious festivals" and ends "But let justice roll on like a river, righteousness like a never-failing stream!" (For the moment, skip over the intervening two oracles; they will be recommended for further reading and discussion at the end of this session.)

In oracle A above, God says that he wants justice *rather than* insincere worship. In this oracle the language is much stronger. God says that he *hates* and *despises* worship that's offered by people who are oppressing others. It offends him so much that it's like a "stench."

⮑ To appreciate how Amos's words struck his original listeners, substitute the names of contemporary religious practices for the ones listed in this oracle. (For example, "I hate, I despise your worship gatherings, your small groups are a stench to me.") What's the impact when you do this? How bad do you think a group of people needs to get before God begins to feel this way about their worship?

3 Have someone read the next oracle, which begins "Did you bring me sacrifices and offerings" and ends "says the LORD, whose name is God Almighty." (It's been placed here because it also talks about sacrifices.)

Amos once again challenges the Israelites' complacency in their covenant relationship with God. They may be the "family that God brought up out of Egypt," but even on the journey away from Egypt they started worshipping other gods. They've been unfaithful right from the start, so they have no grounds to expect God to deliver them from conquest and exile.

⮑ Is your country considered a Christian nation that's entitled to special blessings from God? If so, through what means is this belief proclaimed? How much truth is there to the claim? What would happen to a public figure who asserted that the country was not a Christian nation, that this was a fiction that had been used to excuse unjust actions over the years, and that many things needed to change or the country should expect judgment rather than blessing from God?

4 Have someone read the next oracle, which begins "Woe to you who are complacent in Zion" and ends "your feasting and lounging will end." (This oracle is placed here because, like the preceding one, it challenges the people's complacency and ends with a prediction of exile. Amos addresses the kingdom of Judah along with the kingdom of Israel.)

This is the oracle noted in session 1 where Amos uses the same Hebrew term to describe how those who consider themselves the *foremost* nation, and who use the *finest* lotions, will be the *first* to go into exile. At this time Israel controlled the Aramean cities of Kalneh and Hamath; Judah controlled the Philistine city of **Gath**. But if these territories could be conquered, Amos asks, why not Israel and Judah themselves—what's the difference? The people of Judah may have felt, as one of their psalms would put it, that "Mount Zion . . . cannot be shaken but endures forever," and the people of Israel may have had similar confidence about their capital of Samaria. But their lifestyle of callous, self-indulgent consumption made them prime targets for impending divine judgment.

This prophecy was partially fulfilled in 722 BC when the resurgent Assyrian empire conquered Samaria and carried its people off into exile. The kingdom of Judah was spared because it responded to the warnings of the prophet Micah, whose words you'll consider later in this guide. However, this was only a temporary reprieve. Eventually Judah abandoned God's ways once again and was conquered and exiled by the Babylonians in 587 BC.

⮑ Identify the places in this oracle where Amos describes furniture, rich foods, media entertainment, alcohol, and cosmetics.

In a typical evening of television watching, how often would you see each of these things advertised? Is this spiritually dangerous?

FOR FURTHER READING AND DISCUSSION

- The two oracles that directly follow the chiasm depict the coming judgment. The first describes how the land will be filled with wailing; the second uses dangerous animals to symbolize how there will be no escape. It says, at its beginning and end, that the "day of the LORD," when the people expect God to give them victory over their enemies, will actually be a time of "darkness, not light." Do you know people who are eagerly awaiting the end of the world, expecting God's vindication? Will the "day of the LORD" have a dark side that we should perhaps not be so eager for?

- The oracle after the last one you considered for this session—it begins "The Sovereign LORD has sworn by himself"—contains similar language to the earlier one about worship. It uses the terms *abhor* and *detest* to describe God's feelings towards the fortresses the people are so proud of. If God is love, how can Amos say that he hates like this?

- In the next oracle, Amos uses questions to lead his listeners to a conclusion: Some things don't belong in certain places. ("Does one plow the sea with oxen?") It should be obvious to the Israelites that corruption doesn't belong where there should be justice, but in the hubris of their recent conquests, they can't recognize this. What things are out of place in your society? What keeps people from noticing?

AMOS DESCRIBES HIS VISIONS FROM GOD AND HIS EXPULSION FROM ISRAEL

Book of Amos > Visions and Expulsion Narrative

INTRODUCTION

Amos records several visions he saw of impending judgment. These are placed near the end of the book, even though they were probably what first motivated him to go and warn the people of Israel. The account of Amos's expulsion and some additional oracles have been placed among these vision reports because of similarities in their language.

READING AND DISCUSSION

1 Have four people read the first four vision reports. They all begin something like, "This is what the Sovereign LORD showed me." Skip over the expulsion account for now. (In these reports Amos sometimes calls the Israelites "Jacob" or "Isaac," after their ancestors.)

The first two visions are of disasters that threaten to destroy the land. Amos intercedes for the people and God agrees to spare them. We don't know how much time passes before Amos sees his third and fourth visions, but during this time Israel persists in oppression and corruption until God has to say, "I will spare them no longer."

These later visions communicate symbolically. A plumb line was used to ensure that a wall was straight; if Israel were a wall, the line would show that it was crooked. The word for "ripe fruit" in Hebrew sounds very much like the word for "end"; God says literally to Amos, "The *end* has come for my people Israel." (Because this play on the sound of the words can't be reproduced in English, the NIV translates the sense of the words to show this connection: "The time is *ripe* for my people Israel.")

⟳ Amos's prayers seem to persuade God, at least temporarily, not to carry out judgments he has decided upon. Do you believe that prayer can do this? If so, what individuals or groups most need your prayers right now? At what point does praying for people cease to be effective and judgment becomes inevitable?

⟳ Why do you think God communicates with Amos through visual symbols and word plays in the third and fourth visions? (Why not show him further scenes of disaster?)

2 The expulsion account is placed after the third vision report because both speak of God using a sword against King Jereboam. Have three people read this account like a play, taking these parts:

- Narrator
- Amaziah
- Amos

This account gives us just about all the information we have about Amos personally except for what we're told at the start of the book. Amaziah thinks that Amos is a prophet-for-hire who somehow doesn't realize that his predictions of Israel's doom will find a better-paying audience in the rival southern kingdom of Judah. Amos counters that he's not looking for money; he's only here because God has sent him. Amaziah will recognize that he's a genuine prophet when the disasters Amos is predicting overtake him and his family.

⟳ If Amos had had the opportunity to apprentice with another prophet before coming north to Israel, do you think he would have been more effective or less effective in his mission? Explain your answer.

⮑ Is it fair for Amaziah's wife and children to suffer the fate Amos predicts for them because of Amaziah's resistance to God?

3 Have someone read the oracle that follows the fourth vision report, beginning "Hear this, you who trample the needy" and ending "I will make . . . the end of it like a bitter day." (The fourth vision report predicts that "the songs in the temple will turn to wailing"; this oracle follows because in it God says, "I will turn your religious festivals into mourning and all your singing into weeping.")

Amos describes more of the greed and oppression that are corrupting the kingdom of Israel and then announces an ominous sign of God's judgment against them: an earthquake. The opening of the book tells us there was an earthquake in Israel two years after Amos spoke there. This oracle then says God will "darken the earth in broad daylight." This is possibly a prediction of an eclipse, but if it is, the book says nothing about it being fulfilled. It's more likely a symbol for judgment; this image occurs often in Amos's oracles (for example, "the day of the LORD . . . will be darkness, not light"). The descriptions of mourning that follow are more clearly realistic.

⮑ The merchants Amos describes are cheating outright: giving less than full measure, using dishonest scales, diluting the good grain with swept-up spillage, violating the Sabbath ban on business, etc. But are similar practices permissible if they're not strictly dishonest: expanding business hours, reducing quantities without changing the packaging, diluting the advertised product with cheaper ingredients, etc.? Is it simply up to the customer to figure out what's going on and beware? Or are merchants responsible before God for a certain degree of transparency and generosity, even if this lowers their profits?

⮑ The merchants in Israel made food so unaffordable that the poor had to sell themselves into slavery. Where in the world today do people have to give up their freedom in order to survive? What organizations do you know that are working to help such people? How can your group support their work?

⮑ In session 3 you discussed different perspectives on natural disasters. Does the fact that Amos predicted the earthquake that struck Israel at this time make you more inclined to see it as a direct expression of divine judgment?

The next oracle ("The days are coming") and the fifth vision report ("I saw the Lord standing by the altar") will be recommended for further reading and discussion.

4 The last stanza of the song you've encountered twice before follows the fifth vision report. This stanza begins, "The Lord, the LORD Almighty." Find the other two stanzas (you were asked in sessions 3 and 4 to note their locations) and have different people now read the three song stanzas in turn.

The oracles in the book of Amos offer words of warning; this song turns those words into worship. It praises God as the creator who also has the power to undo the order of creation through flood, earthquake, and darkness. This song, whether written by Amos himself or by someone his work inspired, lifts its focus from the crimes of the Israelites to the character of the God whose purposes they are abandoning. One of the greatest tragedies for the Israelites was that they never understood what they could have had in place of the corruption and greed that ultimately destroyed them. This song gives us a brief glimpse into the appreciation for God's beauty and majesty that escaped them.

⮑ Many songs and hymns today praise God as the Creator. But is it also appropriate to praise God for his destructive power? Explain your answer.

⮑ Say whether you agree or disagree with the following statement, and why: "If we only knew who God really was, we'd never choose anything he didn't approve of."

5 Skip for now down to the last oracle in the book and have someone read this for the group. It begins, "In that day I will restore David's fallen shelter." (This means the tabernacle or temple in Jerusalem as a symbol for the whole nation.)

As we'll see more clearly in the sessions ahead, the oracles of the prophets alternate between warnings of ruin and promises of restoration. In the book of Amos there's only one oracle of restoration, at the very end. But it does make wonderful promises of renewed community, prosperity, and joy.

➲ If you can, tell the group about a person or institution that you've seen God restore to health and flourishing after they took a bad course that had destructive consequences. Do you think God always tries to bring restoration after ruin? Or does a point come when God says, "There's nothing more I can do for you"? Why would God want to restore the Israelites after they did all the things Amos describes in his oracles?

FOR FURTHER READING AND DISCUSSION

• After the oracle about the merchants there's one that describes a coming "famine of hearing the words of the Lord." The Israelites will have ignored God's messengers so stubbornly that he will stop speaking to them. What would it look like if God stopped speaking to the people of your culture? What channels of communication would shut down?

• Amos reports a fifth vision in which he was in a temple and "saw the Lord standing by the altar," ordering the collapse of the temple as the beginning of the disasters that would overtake all the people, no matter how they tried to escape. If Amos was in the temple at Bethel when he had this vision and if he described it out loud at the time, what would have been the effect on those who heard him?

• The oracle that follows the third song stanza ("Are not you Israelites the same to me as the Cushites?") mentions the island of Caphtor (Crete). The fifth vision report describes the "tops of the pillars"; the word for these in Hebrew is *caphtor*. That's why these materials have been placed close together.

This oracle offers a final challenge to the Israelites' false sense of security in their covenant relationship with God. Sure, Amos says, God brought you out of Egypt, but he also brought other nations into their present lands from other places, so what makes you any different? Through their disobedience, the Israelites are nullifying the effects of the foundational redemptive event of the First Testament—the exodus. The equivalent today would be someone thinking they could sin with impunity because Jesus died on the cross for them. A modern-day Amos might challenge them by saying, "Lots of people die! If you persistently disobey and ignore God, then Jesus' death has no more value for you than anyone else's death might have for another person." What would you think of such a statement?

FOR YOUR NEXT MEETING

Group members should read the introduction to Hosea in *The Books of the Bible* to prepare for session 6. At the start of your next meeting give them a chance to ask any questions they have about this introduction. You can also read the introduction in your group and discuss it before doing the session.

HOSEA

OUTLINE OF HOSEA

While the book of Amos consists of about thirty short compositions that are loosely arranged, the material in Hosea is more formally arranged into two parts, reflecting two different time periods:

1. The first part of the book (which you will consider in session 7) is set during the prosperous reign of Jereboam II. It uses the story of Hosea's marriage as an illustration of God's love for Israel. The story is told in two narrative episodes, with an oracle in between.

2. The second part reflects the chaotic conditions of the years after Jereboam died. It is much longer and consists entirely of oracles. It's made up of two thematically defined sections.

    a. In the first section (sessions 8 and 9), God says he has a "charge to bring" against the people of Israel. Groups of thematically related oracles then present the evidence that the nation has broken its covenant with God:

      • Israel's leaders have been setting a bad example instead of teaching God's laws (beginning with "Hear the word of the LORD, you Israelites")

      • Social injustice and political intrigues are corroding the society ("Sound the trumpet in Gibeah, the horn in Ramah")

      • Israel is depending on foreign powers instead of trusting in the LORD ("Ephraim mixes with the nations")

      The section concludes with a summation ("Do not rejoice, Israel") that announces judgment against the nation for rejecting God's covenant—and for rejecting Hosea as his prophet.

    b. The second section (session 10) makes the case against Israel from another perspective, by retracing the history of its relationship with God ("When I found Israel, it was like finding grapes in the desert"). It ends with a call to the people of Hosea's time ("Return, Israel, to the LORD your God") and with an admonition to later readers to reflect carefully on its words.

EXPERIENCING THE BOOK OF HOSEA AS A WHOLE

Before doing this session, give group members the chance to ask questions and share their reflections about the introduction to Hosea in The Books of the Bible.

INTRODUCTION

In this session you'll read the whole book of Hosea together. This will prepare you to consider its individual sections in the sessions ahead.

While we don't know much about Hosea, the book does give us a few clues about who he was:

- The heading identifies the kings who reigned while he spoke to Israel. We can determine from this information that Hosea was active from about the 750s to the 720s BC, a generation after Amos. (The heading also tells us his father's name, although this doesn't help us identify him much further.)

- The Hebrew text of Hosea's words is full of difficult and uncertain readings. Most scholars conclude from this that he was a native of the northern kingdom of Israel and spoke its distinctive dialect, as the scribes in Judah seem to have had trouble understanding his words when they received them for safekeeping and transmission after Israel was conquered.

(The difficulty of the text has led scholars to suggest different readings in many places. This guide will note these suggestions as alternatives to the NIV translation when they can help make sense of Hosea's words.)

- At the start of the book, Hosea tells how he married a woman named Gomer and how they were separated and then reconciled. (We'll explore this more in the next session.) As a result, paradoxically, while we know relatively little about Hosea's public life, we're given a privileged glimpse into his private life and we see how it illustrates God's love for the wayward nation of Israel.

READING

Have members of your group who are good at reading out loud and who enjoy doing so take turns reading through the book, switching whenever they come to what feels like a natural break. This should take about twenty minutes. As you listen, you can follow how the book unfolds by looking at the outline on p. 38.

You'll find Hosea right after Amos in *The Books of the Bible*, in which the prophetic books are placed in their likely historical order. In most other editions, Hosea comes a couple of books before Amos.[1]

Hosea is known for his striking, compact images. (For example: "Your love is like the morning mist"; "Their hearts are like an oven" that "smolders all night"; The king will be "swept away like a twig on the surface of the waters.") Listen for images like these as the book is being read and consider their impact.

---

1. Hosea comes two books before Amos in the traditional order because the first several shorter prophetic books were arranged by the same principle that's used for oracles within books like Amos. If the language at the end of one book was reminiscent of the language in another book, the second book was placed after the first. Specifically, because it says near the end of Hosea, "Return, Israel, to the LORD your God," and Joel says, "'Even now,' declares the LORD, 'return to me with all your heart,'" Joel follows Hosea—even though it may have been composed centuries later. Because Joel then says that "the LORD will roar from Zion and thunder from Jerusalem," and the book of Amos begins with almost this same phrase, Amos follows Joel—even though Amos likely came centuries earlier.

DISCUSSION

⊃ What things struck you most as you listened to the book of Hosea? What were your favorite parts? Which parts did you have more trouble connecting with? Why?

⊃ Which images in the book had the most impact for you? Why?

⊃ Before you did this session, what would you have told someone who asked you, "So, what's Hosea about?" How would you answer that question now? What does the book of Hosea have to say to people today?

⊃ Compare the experience of listening to Hosea with that of listening to Amos. As noted earlier, Amos communicates through a scattering of short compositions, comparable to today's blog posts and Twitter feeds. Hosea communicates through longer, more developed oracles that are formally organized within the book— something more like Shakespeare's sonnets. What for you are the strengths and limitations of each form of communication?

SESSION 7

HOSEA'S LOVE FOR HIS WIFE DEMONSTRATES GOD'S LOVE FOR HIS UNFAITHFUL PEOPLE

Book of Hosea > First Part

INTRODUCTION

As you saw last time, the book of Hosea begins with two stories about his marriage.[1] An oracle in between uses the circumstances of the marriage to represent God's relationship with the people of Israel. In this session you'll explore these passages in more detail.

---

1.   While many interpreters believe that Hosea marries, separates from, and is reconciled to the same woman, others hold that he marries two different women (which was permitted in this culture). English translations vary, reflecting these divergent views. While both understandings can be defended from the text, in this study guide we will follow the interpretation that the second story describes Hosea being reconciled with the same woman he marries in the first story, as reflected in the NIV translation, "The LORD said to me, 'Go, show your love to your wife again.'"

READING AND DISCUSSION

1 Have someone read the first story about Hosea's marriage and the brief prediction of Israel's restoration that follows, ending with "Say of your brothers, 'My people,' and of your sisters, 'My loved one.'"

God tells Hosea to marry a "promiscuous woman," literally a "woman of prostitution." Some interpreters believe that this means Gomer is a prostitute. Others consider this less likely, since she's apparently still living in the house of her father Diblaim. The expression may refer instead to how she will eventually be unfaithful to Hosea. Or, it may describe how she, like the rest of the country, is caught up in a "spirit of prostitution," that is, unfaithfulness to the LORD. In that case Hosea is to marry a woman whose character and conduct mirror that of the nation at large.

Whatever the explanation, in this first story it's not Hosea's marriage that serves as a prophetic sign. It's the names of his children. These names depict the consequences Israel will soon experience for turning away from the LORD and worshipping Baal. The news of a child's birth and name would spread widely by word of mouth in this culture, making this another effective means of communicating God's message.

Hosea is to call his first son **Jezreel**, after the city where, nearly a century earlier, Jereboam's great-grandfather Jehu slaughtered the ruling dynasty of Israel and claimed the throne for himself and his descendants. God will soon avenge this massacre and Jehu's dynasty will come to an end. Then the nation will suffer a catastrophic defeat in the nearby **Valley of Jezreel** (which the invading Assyrians will follow inland from the coast; see the map on p. 8). Israel will be conquered and exiled. All of this will express how the nation has broken its covenant with the LORD, so that they have become "not loved" and "not [his] people," as the names of Hosea's other two children indicate.

⮑ God tells Hosea to marry a woman who may be a prostitute, and who at least doesn't share his faith and will be unfaithful to him. In any case, this isn't in keeping with God's proper intentions for marriage. God then tells Hosea to give his children names with negative meanings. It seems almost like child abuse to give someone a name that will expose them to ridicule and destroy their self-esteem. (Imagine going through life being called Not Loved!) Are God's larger purposes—to rescue his covenant relationship with the ancient nation of Israel, through which he's trying to reach the rest of the world—so important that they justify extraordinary measures like these, whatever suffering they cause for Hosea and his family? Could similar extraordinary measures be justified today? Explain your answer.

⮑ The story does end with a hopeful promise in which God gives a positive meaning to the name Jezreel and changes the other two names to "My people" and "My loved one." It's possible that Hosea was supposed to change the names of his younger two children to illustrate the certainty of this promise. Do you have a negative name stuck in your head from things people have said to you or things that have happened to you? Consciously choose a positive name for yourself to replace this negative one, as God does for Hosea's children here. What effect does this have on you?

2 In this culture, when two parties made a covenant and one party then broke it, the other party would conduct a lawsuit (known as a *rib* in Hebrew) either to get them to honor the covenant or to establish that they were no longer bound to keep their own part of the agreement. In the oracle that follows the first story about Hosea, God conducts a *rib* against the nation of Israel, depicting himself as an aggrieved husband whose wife has broken their marriage covenant. The oracle alternates back and forth between more literal descriptions of the situation in Israel and more metaphorical descriptions of the troubled marriage.

The husband cites the evidence for his wife's unfaithfulness—she's even had children by other men—and argues that he's not bound to care for these children, nor to give his wife liberty to go about, or even to provide for her anymore, since she's been taking gifts from her lovers. It appears that the *rib* will inevitably culminate in the husband demanding a divorce. Instead, there's a surprise. He announces that, through the restrictive measures he has described, he will get his wife alone, "allure her" and "speak tenderly to her," and win back her heart. In the end, he will even adopt her children as his own. All of this symbolically depicts the purposes God will be pursuing when he sends the people into exile in order to regain their devotion so he can ultimately restore them to their land.

Have someone read this oracle, beginning with "Rebuke your mother, rebuke her, for she is not my wife" and ending "they will say, 'You are my God.'"

⮑ This oracle is essentially about God using adverse circumstances to restore a community's devotion. Do you know of any communities of Jesus' followers that have been brought back to a deeper devotion to God through circumstances of trouble or need? If so, tell their story.

⮑ The oracle is also compelling on the figurative level for the story it tells of a restored marriage. Do you know anyone who had grounds for divorce but who chose to pursue reconciliation instead? Share, if you can, what happened when they did.

⮑ If this oracle is meant to inform our understanding of Hosea's story, then it's possible he wasn't the father of all of Gomer's children. The text leaves this possibility open, saying that she "bore him a son" but that she then "gave birth to a daughter" and "had another son." This would make the names "Not Loved" and "Not My People" open repudiations of these children. But if we continue to take the oracle as our guide to the story, Hosea would ultimately adopt these children and change their names to "My Loved One" and "My People." Do you know any followers of Jesus who are raising children who aren't their own offspring? (For example, people who have adopted, or who have married single or divorced parents.) How are they able to communicate God's love and acceptance to these children by treating them as their own?

3 Have someone read the second story about Hosea's marriage, beginning with "The LORD said to me, 'Go, show your love to your wife again'" and ending with "They will come trembling to the LORD and to his blessings in the last days."

Hosea now lives out, as a prophetic sign, the drama that God presents figuratively in the oracle. Gomer has apparently left him for another man. She has perhaps become his concubine, or he may have sold her into slavery, because Hosea has to purchase her back. He does this partly in cash and partly in grain, which was acceptable in trade; this may represent how Hosea will provide for her needs once more, reversing the aggrieved husband's decision in the oracle to withhold the provisions he had been giving to his wife.

Hosea is now Gomer's master as well as her husband, so she must obey his orders. He requires her to be chaste and states that the two of them will not have sexual relations at first. On a symbolic level, this represents how the Israelites will go into exile and be without any of the tokens of their covenant relationship with God. But in the real-life story, this season of abstinence has an important message for Gomer. In her recent experience, the only thing men have wanted from her is sex. If they've given her anything, it was to get this in return. Now a man will love and care for her unconditionally. This is a picture of God's love for Gomer, for Israel, and for everyone who hears her story.

And we have reason to believe that the sexual relationship was ultimately restored. The LORD tells Israel in the oracle that one day "you will call me 'my husband'; you will no longer call me 'my master.'" The name Baal means "master," and on a symbolic level this is a prediction that Israel will stop worshipping Baal and turn back to the LORD. But if the oracle truly parallels Hosea's own story, then we can conclude that once Gomer understood and appreciated his love for her, they spent the rest of their days together not as master and servant, but as husband and wife in every sense.

⮑ The story of Hosea's relationship with Gomer illustrates God's love for people. Have you ever gotten or been given the impression that God wanted a relationship with you because he wanted something from you? Does hearing this story help you understand the unconditional nature of God's love better?

➲ Many women (and children) are sexually trafficked today, as Gomer likely was. Whether they run away from their husbands or parents, are enticed with false promises, or are abducted, they are brought into a life in which they are valued only as objects of sex. Have you heard the story of anyone who was rescued from this life and shown the love of God by followers of Jesus? If so, share the story with the group if you can. What can you and your group do to support those who are seeking to rescue and restore people who have been sexually trafficked?

HOSEA ACCUSES THE NATION'S LEADERS AND WARNS OF COMING JUDGMENT

Book of Hosea > Second Part > First Section

INTRODUCTION

The first part of the book of Hosea, which you considered last time, takes place during the secure and prosperous reign of Jereboam II. It speaks of Israel having grain, new wine, olive oil, silver, and gold. The oracles in the rest of the book come from the chaotic years after Jereboam's death. Then the nation had a succession of weak kings who each reigned only a short time; many were assassinated. These oracles depict a situation of social disintegration, banditry, and shortages ("the land dries up, and all who live in it waste away").

As noted in session 6, this next part of the book has two main sections. In this session you'll begin considering its first section, in which God brings charges against the Israelites for breaking their covenant with him.

READING AND DISCUSSION

1 Have different people read the next four oracles in the book, beginning at these places:

- "Hear the word of the LORD, you Israelites"
- "My people consult a wooden idol"

- "Though you, Israel, commit adultery, do not let Judah become guilty"
- "Hear this, you priests! Pay attention, you Israelites!" (ending, "When they celebrate their New Moon feasts, he will devour their fields")

God announces at the beginning of the first oracle that he has a charge (*rîb*) to bring against the Israelites. He describes how people have been breaking the Ten Commandments to illustrate how the nation as a whole has broken its covenant with him.

Ordinarily a priest, as God's representative, would bring this charge against the people. But the oracle then says, in a probable alternative reading, that God doesn't want any priest to do this, "for my charge is against you, O priest!" (NIV "your people are like those who bring charges against a priest"). Instead of teaching the people and setting a good example, the priests are ignoring the law and destroying their own people (NIV "mother"). And so God says he will punish priest and people alike.

The next oracle addresses a second group that was supposed to provide guidance and set a proper example: fathers, who were the moral and legal authorities in the family in this culture. They had a particular responsibility to guard the purity of their daughters and daughters-in-law (who would come to live in their households). The young women of Israel were instead engaging in prostitution and committing adultery, but God says shockingly that he will not punish them. Why? Because their fathers are doing the same things. The nation is being corrupted morally because those who are supposed to be setting a good example are setting a bad one instead.

The next two oracles warn that sacred sites like Gilgal and Bethel (which Hosea calls Beth Aven, "house of wickedness" instead of "house of God") have become centers of drunkenness and immorality because they're now devoted to the fertility cult of Baal. They are places of prostitution, by which Hosea means both unfaithfulness to God spiritually and commercial sex physically. And so, like Amos, he warns people to stay away from these sites, because "when they go . . . to seek the Lord, they will not find him; he has withdrawn himself from them."

⊃ When God says "like people, like priests," this isn't a compliment. Israel's priests were supposed to meet a higher standard of conduct than the average person. What types of leaders does your society expect to meet a higher standard? How successfully do they do this? What happens when they don't? Name at least one national leader whose moral example you respect and admire.

⊃ (Let the women and men in your group discuss the following questions separately if they'd be more comfortable that way.) For the women: What did your father do, or what do you wish he'd done, to show you that sex is something good and pure that belongs only in marriage? For the men: How can men show their daughters and the other young women in their lives that sex is something good and pure that belongs only in marriage? What lifestyle choices do men need to make in order to have credibility when they try to communicate this message? (If the women and men discussed these questions separately, have a spokesperson for each group summarize their conclusions when everyone gets back together.)

2 Have different people read the next five oracles in the book, beginning at these places:

- "Sound the trumpet in Gibeah"
- "Ephraim is oppressed, trampled in judgment"
- "Come, let us return to the LORD"
- "What can I do with you, Ephraim?"
- "As at Adam, they have broken the covenant" (ending, "All their kings fall, and none of them calls on me")

This next group of oracles continues the charge against Israel by describing the injustices and crimes that are spreading throughout the land: property theft (moving boundary stones), highway robbery, swindling, breaking and entering, banditry. As Hosea depicts these crimes, he declares that the people have "broken the covenant" and been unfaithful to God. The oracles also expose the power struggles and political intrigues behind the recurring royal assassinations that have left the nation weak and directionless ("they devour their rulers," "all their kings fall"). But these oracles also begin to announce God's judgment against the nation.

In one sense this judgment is already occurring, through the decay and corruption that are slowly destroying the society. Hosea compares it to a moth eating holes in a garment and rot decomposing a fabric. But in another sense, the judgment is still to come, and it will be dramatic: Hosea compares it to a flood and the attack of a lion. Both of these images are also found in the book of Amos; Hosea may be alluding to his predecessor intentionally to show that he's continuing his mission. (There are many other echoes of Amos in this book, for example, "the land dries up," "do not go to Gilgal," "I will send fire on their cities that will consume their fortresses," etc.) "I cut you in pieces with my prophets" is a more direct reference to Amos and others who have apparently tried to warn Israel, but without success.

At one point Hosea pleads directly with his fellow Israelites, "Come, let us return to the LORD." But he gets only a faint, temporary response. Israel's love for God is "like the morning mist, like the early dew that disappears." The people feel some regret for a little while, but then they go right back to what they've been doing. And so the remedy must be drastic: conquest and exile. "Ephraim" (another name for Israel) "will be laid waste on the day of reckoning."

⮑ Is the spread of crime and gang activity, such as Hosea describes, the first stage in social disintegration? Can escalation be prevented, and neighborhoods and cities reclaimed, by cracking down on petty crime (the so-called "broken windows" theory)? If so, why does this work?

⮑ Hosea describes how the people of Israel are stuck in a cycle of destructive behavior, temporary regret, and renewed destructive behavior. Do you think that experiencing negative consequences like the ones Hosea predicts is the only way for a person to break out of such a cycle? Why or why not?

GOD FINDS ISRAEL GUILTY OF COVENANT-BREAKING AND PASSES SENTENCE

Book of Hosea > Second Part > First Section, Concluded

INTRODUCTION

In this session you'll finish considering the first section of the second part of Hosea, in which God brings charges against the Israelites for breaking their covenant and announces the judgment that's coming on them as a result.

READING

Have different people read the next four oracles in the book, beginning at these places:

- "Ephraim mixes with the nations"
- "Put the trumpet to your lips!"
- "Israel is swallowed up; now she is among the nations"
- "Do not rejoice, Israel; do not be jubilant like the other nations" (ending, "God will remember their wickedness and punish them for their sins")

DISCUSSION

1 These oracles present the final piece of evidence that Israel has broken its covenant with the LORD. We've already heard how its leaders and people have been violating God's commandments, spreading crime and injustice throughout the society, and how they've been worshipping Baal with drunkenness and immorality. Now Hosea documents how they've also been depending for security and protection on foreign powers instead of the LORD. This would be bad enough in itself, but they haven't even been doing it very well.

The new kings who have come to the throne through rebellion and assassination have typically reversed the policies of their predecessors, so that Israel has shifted continually between appeasing the Assyrian empire and identifying with the rebellious coalitions Egypt has been trying to stir up. As Hosea puts it, "Ephraim is like a dove, easily deceived and senseless—now calling to Egypt, now turning to Assyria." Fittingly, when Israel is finally judged for its unfaithfulness to God, some of its population will be carried off to Egypt while the rest of it will be exiled to Assyria. The people who wanted to "mix with the nations" instead of belonging distinctively to the LORD will get their wish.

⤳ The people of God on earth are no longer a single nation; they're the multinational community of Jesus' followers. This community is much more of a network than a hierarchy, so it's known and experienced primarily through its local expressions (churches). These are "mixed with the nations" in the sense that they're scattered among all the countries of the world, but they're still supposed to belong distinctively to God and not depend on earthly powers. What things might your church be tempted to depend on instead of God? How can it recognize this danger and avoid it? How would you answer these questions for yourself as an individual believer? (If you're not a follower of Jesus, you can still respond based on your observations of other followers and their churches.)

2 God's *rib* against the Israelites culminates in these oracles with a verdict of guilty. "The people have broken my covenant and rebelled against my law," the LORD declares, telling Israel, "You have been unfaithful to your

God." Even though Israel is crumbling, not even this is bringing it back to the covenant: "Despite all this he does not return to the LORD his God." (This is another echo of Amos: "Yet you have not returned to me.")

As the verdict is delivered, sentence is also passed. Hosea has already said several times that Israel will be punished through conquest and exile, but now he expresses this in the specific language of God's historic covenant with Israel. In the last great speech Moses gave to the nation, recorded in the book of Deuteronomy, he described the curses Israel would experience if it broke its covenant with the LORD. Hosea echoes several of these curses here:

- Moses said, "The LORD will bring a nation against you from far away . . . like an eagle swooping down." Hosea cries, "An eagle is over the house of the LORD."
- Moses told the people they would "sow much seed" but "harvest little" and that foreigners would "leave you no grain, new wine or olive oil." Hosea says, "The stalk has no head; it will produce no flour. Were it to yield grain, foreigners would swallow it up."
- Moses told the people they would flee before their enemies; Hosea says, "Israel has rejected what is good; an enemy will pursue him."
- Moses warned, "The LORD will send you back . . . to Egypt"; Hosea declares, "Ephraim will return to Egypt."

In this way Hosea identifies the troubles the Israelites are already experiencing, and the much worse ones that will soon follow, as the consequences of their covenant-breaking.

⮑ Even though the Bible was not complete in Hosea's day and the existing Scriptures were largely transmitted orally rather than in writing, Hosea knows the story of God well enough to recognize how the people of God are continuing it in his day. Unfortunately, they're doing so negatively, so that the story will have to take a darker turn before it can have a new beginning. How is the story of God progressing in your own place and time? If you're part of a community of Jesus' followers, what would you say it's doing to continue the story positively towards its intended culmination, as you understand it?

3 Hosea appears to have delivered the fourth oracle you read for this session at a festival the people were celebrating at one of the sacred sites in Israel. He tells them not to rejoice, because soon they won't be able to hold these festivals anymore. When the "feast days of the LORD" come around each year, the survivors of Israel will be trapped in exile and unable to come and observe them. The sacred sites will become overgrown with thorns and briers.

This oracle may be one of the last Hosea ever delivered in person to the nation of Israel. It provides a fitting conclusion to God's *rib* against Israel because it also describes the conclusion of Hosea's mission. The people haven't heeded his warnings or his call to return to the LORD; instead, they consider him a fool and a maniac. They've even threatened him: "The prophet . . . is the watchman over Ephraim, yet snares await him on all his paths, and hostility in the house of his God." Once the people will no longer listen to his messenger, there's nothing more God can do to reach them. Judgment has become inevitable.

⟳ Answer the following questions as you think Hosea would have: How did it feel to be called a fool and a maniac for delivering God's message? What concerns did you have for your own safety? What led you to conclude the people ultimately wouldn't listen to you? Why did you decide to give one last oracle at a festival at a sacred site? When you look back over the years you spent as a prophet, would you say they were worth it?

FOR YOUR NEXT MEETING

Make sure that pencils and paper are available for each group member to do some simple drawings as a reflection exercise.

SESSION 10

GOD RECALLS THE BEGINNINGS OF HIS RELATIONSHIP WITH ISRAEL

Book of Hosea > Second Part > Second Section

INTRODUCTION

The rest of the book of Hosea (the second section of the second part) presents a series of oracles in which God reviews the history of his relationship with the nation of Israel. These oracles provide another way of reaching the same conclusion as the *rib* or lawsuit you considered in the last two sessions. The method is no longer charges, evidence, and verdict, but retrospective. By repeatedly recalling how the relationship began, Hosea shows the people how far they've wandered from what it's supposed to be.

Some of the oracles in this part of the book appear to reflect events that took place after Hosea moved to Judah for his safety. Others may come from earlier times in his life. As a whole, they've been collected and placed at the end of the book because they tell the story of Israel's relationship with God, and readers of Hosea's words can still become part of that story even after the nation is conquered and exiled. Indeed, the story continues down to the present day, when the people of God have become the multinational community of Jesus' followers that is open to readers everywhere in the world.

READING

Have different people read the next four oracles in the book, beginning at these places:

- "When I found Israel, it was like finding grapes in the desert"
- "Israel was a spreading vine"
- "Since the days of Gibeah you have sinned, Israel"
- "When Israel was a child, I loved him" (ending, "'I will settle them in their homes,' declares the LORD")

(The third oracle mentions an invader named Shalman. This may be either of the two Assyrian emperors named Shalmaneser who conquered Israelite territory at various points. This Shalman is guilty of the same kind of atrocities in warfare that Amos condemns in the extended opening oracle of his book.)

DISCUSSION

1 Each of these oracles presents an extended image of organic growth and development. But each oracle then depicts this growth failing to reach its intended end: It either gets arrested or misdirected.

- The first oracle develops the image of fertility: conception, pregnancy, birth, nursing. But it then declares that all these things will be taken away from Israel, as an ironic judgment on the people for their devotion to the fertility god Baal.
- The second oracle presents an image of growing plants, but these turn out to be poisonous rather than good for food. This symbolizes how the king and royal officials are corrupt and the centers of worship are devoted to idolatry. So in the end the only plants in the land will be thorns and thistles. The king will be swept away like a dry twig.
- The third oracle depicts plowing, sowing, and reaping, but then explains that the people have planed wickedness, reaped evil, and eaten the fruit of deception. In consequence, they will be destroyed by invaders.
- The fourth oracle portrays child-rearing: God teaches Israel to walk, holding him up by the arms as he takes his first steps. But

Israel uses this new ability to walk away from God: "The more they were called, the more they went away from me." And so they will be sent away from their land. (However, at the end of this oracle, God resolves to have compassion on the people and bring them back to their homes after this judgment.)

⮑ Following the instructions given here, create a personal spiritual growth and development timeline for yourself by drawing a vine with pencil and paper. Position the paper in landscape format (wider than it is high). Pick an appropriate starting time (for example, when you became a follower of Jesus) and make that the point at which the vine starts growing out of the ground on the bottom left side of the page. Then trace your development across the page to the present day on the right side. Have the vine go upwards during times of growth and progress and go sideways or downwards during seasons of stagnation or decline. Label the various time periods at the bottom of the page. How much have you grown since the start? Have there been seasons of rapid growth? If so, when were they? What things have caused you to plateau or regress? When have you borne the most fruit? (That is, when have you had the greatest influence for God through your words, relationships, roles, and accomplishments?) Draw small grape clusters at these places. What insights do you get from this exercise? If you wish, share your drawing with the group once you've completed it.

⮑ Make a similar drawing of the spiritual development or decline of your nation. Group members should compare and discuss these drawings when they're finished.

2 Three of these oracles also associate various sacred sites, or Israel as a whole, with the locations of some of the most notorious episodes in the nation's early history. This illustrates how the people turned away from God right at the start, as they're continuing to do so in Hosea's day.

- The first oracle describes how the Israelites worshipped Baal at a place called **Baal Peor** just as they were about to enter their new land. (Hosea calls this god Bosheth, meaning "shame"; NIV "that shameful idol.") Hosea compares this incident to their current "wickedness in Gilgal," the drunkenness and immorality they practice at that sacred site. Ironically, it's just across the Jordan River from Baal Peor.

- The third oracle recalls the wickedness of the city of **Gibeah**. When the Israelites first settled in their land, the men of that city tried to gang-rape a man from another tribe who was passing through and, failing this, they raped his concubine to death. When all the other tribes gathered to demand that the perpetrators face justice, the tribe of Benjamin (which contained Gibeah) refused to surrender them. Because Benjamin was militarized and its territory was mountainous and forbidding, a very costly civil war ensued before the criminals were finally captured. Israel in Hosea's time has the same arrogant confidence in its military might, making its royal sanctuary of Bethel a contemporary Gibeah.

- The fourth oracle mentions the cities of Admah and Zeboyim, which were destroyed along with Sodom and Gomorrah for their wickedness during the time of Abraham. Hosea is once again alluding to the curses in Deuteronomy. Moses told the Israelites that if they disobeyed the LORD, their land would become "a burning waste . . . nothing planted, nothing sprouting, no vegetation growing on it. It will be like the destruction of Sodom and Gomorrah, Admah and Zeboyim." This allusion ties together the two main devices in these oracles, the organic growth imagery and the association of present sites with past notorious locations. In this case, however, God is expressing his resolve to rescue the people after they've been punished and corrected through conquest and exile.

➲ What have been some of the most notorious incidents in the life of the community of Jesus' followers? (You can answer based on what you've personally experienced or heard about, or based on what you know from history.) How did these things happen? What has been their effect on the community's reputation and influence? What can the community do to prevent similar things from happening again?

HOSEA FORETELLS ISRAEL'S DESTRUCTION, THEN ANTICIPATES ITS RESTORATION

INTRODUCTION

The book of Hosea ends with more oracles that review the history of God's relationship with Israel and announce impending judgment. However, they're followed by a call for the people to return to God and a promise of restoration. The book ends with an admonition for readers to reflect carefully on everything they've heard.

READING AND DISCUSSION

1 Have someone read the next oracle, beginning with "Ephraim has surrounded me with lies" and ending with "his Lord will . . . repay him for his contempt."

This oracle uses the story of Jacob, the ancestor of the tribes of Israel, as an extended parable or allegory for the history of the nation. The story is offered as narrative evidence in another lawsuit or *rîb* (NIV "charge") that God lodges against the people. In this way the characteristic devices of both sections of the second part of Hosea converge as the book nears its conclusion.

This oracle describes how Jacob was first known as a trickster or deceiver: "He grasped his brother's heel" (that is, to trip him up; the name Jacob is similar to the Hebrew word for "heel"). But the oracle then describes how "as a man he struggled with God," earnestly pursuing his blessing. As a result, Jacob was given a new name, Israel, alluding to this struggle with God. The implications are that the nation now known by this same name should also give up its deception ("the merchant uses dishonest scales and loves to defraud") and earnestly engage God, searching to know what it must do to return to his favor.

The oracle later notes that Jacob/Israel *tended* sheep in a distant country, and it compares this with the way "a prophet" (that is, Moses) *cared for* the nation as it traveled through the wilderness. (The same Hebrew term is used in each case.) The people should recognize that Hosea is fulfilling this protective and caring role in their own day, and they should listen to his warnings from God.

⮑ What does it look like when a person struggles with God to obtain his favor and blessing? Why would someone have to do this? How is a person different after such a struggle?

⮑ Who are the people who have watched out sincerely for your spiritual welfare? Have you listened well to their advice and warnings? If so, how has this helped you? If not, what have been the consequences? How can people identify those God has sent into their lives to care for them in this way, and how can they best benefit from their influence?

2 Have a group member who's willing to handle some difficult material continue the reading, beginning with "When Ephraim spoke, people trembled" and ending with "their little ones will be dashed to the ground, their pregnant women ripped open."

Hosea continues to review the history of Israel's relationship with God, noting events such as its deliverance from slavery in Egypt, God's care for the nation in the wilderness, and the appointment of its first king. However, these events are now recalled not in the hopes of reviving the relationship immediately, but to justify the coming corrective punishment:

- Israel was supposed to serve only the God who brought them out of Egypt; instead, they made and worshipped idols.

- God provided for them, but when they had enough to eat, they forgot him.
- They asked for a human king instead of acknowledging God as their king, and God has now taken this king away.

This oracle probably dates from the years 725–722 BC, after the Assyrian emperor Shalmaneser had captured and imprisoned Israel's last king, Hoshea, for not paying tribute and for seeking an alliance with Egypt. Shalmaneser laid siege to Samaria for these three years and finally conquered the city and exiled the population. By this time Hosea had probably moved down to Judah for his own safety, but he kept speaking to the kingdom of Israel right to the end. This material, probably the latest in the book, is filled with threatening and foreboding. It includes some of the fiercest predictions of judgment, both symbolically ("like a bear robbed of her cubs, I will attack them and rip them open") and literally (the predictions of atrocities at the end).

➲ Even though these atrocities will be committed by the Assyrians, God seems to allow or even prescribe them as a punishment. How can God let infants and unborn children suffer for what the adults in their society have done?

3 Have someone read the last oracle in the book, beginning with "Return, Israel, to the LORD your God" and ending with "I am like a flourishing juniper; your fruitfulness comes from me."

Despite the grim predictions of judgment, the book of Hosea ends (like the book of Amos) on a hopeful note, promising healing and restoration if Israel will return to God. Hosea first suggests what the people should say: They should renounce foreign alliances, confidence in their military power, and idol worship, and seek God's forgiveness and acceptance. God then promises to heal, love, and forgive them. The imagery of growth and development that was used in a sinister way in the oracles you considered last time now returns with a new, positive sense. Agricultural abundance reflects how the nation can flourish once again in a restored relationship with God.

➲ What would it look like for your town, city, or neighborhood to flourish genuinely? What things are currently standing in the way of this? If you're part of a community of Jesus' followers, what is it doing to help overcome these things and bring about greater flourishing? What organizations or conferences do you know that are devoted to this?

4 Finally, have someone read the closing admonition to readers of the book.

⮑ What will you most take to heart and reflect on in the days ahead as a result of your reading and discussion of the book of Hosea?

FOR YOUR NEXT MEETING

Group members should read the introduction to Micah in *The Books of the Bible* to prepare for session 12. (You can also read the introduction in your group and discuss it before doing the session.)

MICAH

OUTLINE OF MICAH

1. First group of oracles (session 13)
   - Judgment, beginning with "Hear, you peoples, all of you"
   - Restoration, beginning with "I will surely gather all of you, Jacob" (one brief oracle)

2. Second group of oracles (session 14)
   - Judgment: "Then I said, 'Listen, you leaders of Jacob'"
   - Restoration: "In the last days the mountain of the LORD's temple will be established"

3. Third group of oracles (session 15)
   - Judgment: "Listen to what the LORD says: 'Stand up, plead my case'"
   - Restoration: "Do not gloat over me, my enemy!"

EXPERIENCING THE BOOK OF MICAH AS A WHOLE

Before doing this session, give group members the chance to ask questions and share their reflections about the introduction to Micah in The Books of the Bible.

This session is relatively short; the next one is longer than usual. If you finish this one early, you can begin the next one in the same meeting.

INTRODUCTION

While Amos and Hosea prophesied in the northern kingdom of Israel, Micah delivered his oracles in the southern kingdom of Judah, although like his predecessors he spoke at times to both kingdoms. We know very little about this prophet except that he lived about a generation after Hosea (based on the dates of the kings named in the book's heading) and that he came from the Judean town of **Moresheth**, near the territory of the Philistines. He probably moved from there to Judah's capital of Jerusalem in order to make his message heard. His family was apparently not prominent, as his father's name isn't mentioned.

The book of Micah begins roughly where the book of Hosea ends, with the Assyrian threat to the city of Samaria in the 720s BC. Micah addresses a number of historical situations from that point forward, at least up to the Assyrian invasion of Judah in 701 BC. His message is essentially the same as that of Amos and Hosea: Israel and Judah are facing God's judgment because of their injustice, oppression, and idol worship. If they don't return to the LORD and do what is right, they'll be chastised by foreign invasion, conquest, and exile.

The book is made up of three groups of oracles. Each one presents oracles of judgment followed by oracles of restoration. Often individual oracles are linked together, as in the book of Amos, by similarities in words, phrases, and images. At the beginning of each group there's a call for the people to hear what God has to say.

READING

In this session you'll read through the whole book of Micah to get an overview that will help you appreciate its individual sections as you consider them in the sessions ahead. Micah comes right after Hosea in *The Books of the Bible*. In most other editions, Micah comes several books later; you can find it in the Table of Contents. As you listen, you can follow how the book unfolds by looking at the outline on p. 66.

Have some members of your group who are good at reading out loud and who enjoy doing so take turns reading through the book, switching whenever they come to what feels like a natural break. This should take about ten or fifteen minutes.

As you're listening to the book, notice the places where Micah alludes to the resistance he's facing as he brings God's word to the people. Also note how he finds renewed strength for this task in his relationship with God. These self-conscious references typically come just as the theme is changing from judgment to restoration within a group of oracles.

DISCUSSION

⮩ Based on your readings of Amos, Hosea, and Micah, how would you say the social conditions in the kingdom of Judah at this time compare with those in the kingdom of Israel? What things in the book of Micah reminded you of things that Amos and Hosea also said? Did you notice any significant differences?

⊃ What would you say is Micah's main message? Can you identify a passage in the book that you feel expresses it concisely?

⊃ Amos and Hosea present mostly oracles of judgment, with brief promises of restoration at the end. In Micah, threats of judgment and promises of restoration alternate throughout. What difference, if any, did this make in your experience of the book?

⊃ God sent Amos to the kingdom of Israel as an untrained foreigner. God called Micah from a humble family in an obscure village to go and speak in the national capital. Hosea was asked to live out the drama of God's relationship with Israel in a troubled marriage. All had to compete with professional "prophets" who were telling the people what they wanted to hear and who tried to silence the true prophets. If you had lived at this time, would you have wanted to be one of God's prophets? Why or why not? What strengths would you have brought to the task? What limitations or lack of apparent qualifications would God have to overcome by empowering your work, as he did for Amos, Hosea, and Micah? (Note: The prophetic role was open to both men and women, as other parts of the Bible show and as Micah himself indicates when he names Miriam as one of Israel's leaders along with Moses and Aaron. So every member of the group can answer these questions.)

MICAH WARNS ISRAEL AND JUDAH OF COMING JUDGMENT FOR OPPRESSION

Book of Micah > First Group of Oracles

INTRODUCTION

The heading to the book of Micah describes its contents as "the vision he saw concerning Samaria and Jerusalem." This summarizes his message by alluding to his two most famous predictions—that the capitals of Israel and Judah would be destroyed by invaders as a divine judgment on their corruption and oppression. The first group of oracles in the book correspondingly begins with one that announces the destruction of Samaria and another that describes an impending threat to Jerusalem, even though Micah probably delivered the first oracle near the beginning of his career and the second one near the end. This opening group of oracles then depicts the oppression in Judah and the people's resistance to Micah's message before ending with a brief promise of restoration.

READING AND DISCUSSION

1 Have someone read the first oracle in the book, beginning with "Hear, you peoples, all of you" and ending with "as the wages of prostitutes they will again be used."

This oracle was delivered some time before Samaria was destroyed in 722 BC. Here Micah pursues a method similar to Hosea's: The oracle is like a *rib* against Israel and Judah. While that specific term isn't used, the LORD says he will bring evidence (NIV "witness") against the peoples of the earth and specifically the citizens of these two kingdoms. In language reminiscent of the song in Amos (which says, "The LORD . . . touches the earth and it melts"), this oracle depicts God coming down to expose and punish the people's corruption. (A depiction like this of God coming into the created world with shattering effects is known as a *theophany*.) Like Hosea, Micah describes the people's worship of Baal as prostitution and predicts that the idolatrous golden images in Israel's temples will become plunder for the invaders. In an ironic judgment, foreign soldiers will take this wealth and spend it on commercial prostitutes.

⮑ Money flowed into Israel's sacred sites as people participated in idolatrous worship and ritual prostitution. Where is the money flowing in your society, and what's attracting it there? What industries are the most profitable? Which are positive and constructive and which are negative and destructive, catering to base instincts and trapping people in addictions? What can followers of Jesus do to promote positive enterprises and discourage negative ones through their patterns of consumption, their advocacy, and their personal example?

2 Have someone read the next oracle, beginning with "Because of this I will weep and wail" and ending with "for they will go from you into exile."

This oracle was delivered around 701 BC as the Assyrians under Sennacherib were invading Judah and threatening Jerusalem. To put down an Egyptian-led rebellion, Sennacherib led an army to the Mediterranean coast and subdued Tyre and Sidon. He next marched south and conquered the Philistine cities of Ashkelon and Ekron, then defeated an Egyptian army near Ekron. This left him free to turn against the kingdom of Judah, the most significant remaining member of the rebel coalition. This oracle traces Sennacherib's progress up the coast, cataloging the cities and towns he overcame on his inexorable march towards Jerusalem. (The exact location of several of these places is unknown, but they are along a route leading northwest from Gath past Moresheth towards Jerusalem. See the map on page 8.)

The oracle is carefully structured, in keeping with the solemnity of its subject. It's an elaborate chiasm that begins and ends with descriptions of mourning. When Micah says he will go about barefoot and naked, this could be meant symbolically, but it may also be a prophetic sign of impending conquest and exile that he acted out. If so, it was as sensational in his day as it would be in our own. (Prophets led interesting lives, to say the least.) In between the descriptions of mourning, the oracle lists twelve locations (a number symbolic of the nation); they're divided into two groups of six by references to the gate of Jerusalem.

The first and last locations are marked by allusions to the story of David, the founder of Judah's ruling dynasty. When Israel's first king Saul and his son Jonathan, David's close friend, were killed by the Philistines, David wrote a lament for them in which he said, "Tell it not in Gath"—don't let the Philistines celebrate this! Saul considered David a threat, so he once had to hide in a cave at Adullam; Micah says that Israel's nobles will have to hide there now. The ten locations in the middle of the oracle are marked by plays on the sound or meaning of their names. For example, the name Ophrah sounds like the Hebrew word for "dust"; Ezel means "companion" or "helper," but it can't help Jerusalem; and so forth. The memorable things Micah says about these locations helps to fix each one as a further benchmark of the Assyrian advance.

⮑ What are the benchmarks that show that an individual or an organization (group, business, government, etc.) has a serious problem? For example, for an individual: missing work, losing friends, spending money on an addictive behavior; for a business: high turnover, declining results, friction among members; etc. On the other hand, what are the benchmarks that show an organization or individual is making positive progress? Use this benchmark approach in the week ahead to evaluate your own life, or to encourage or challenge a friend or an organization you're part of. If you can, think of a way to make each benchmark memorable and compelling.

3 Have someone read the next oracle, beginning with "Woe to those who plan iniquity" and ending with "Therefore you will have no one in the assembly of the LORD to divide the land by lot."

Like Amos and Hosea in Israel, Micah describes how the rich and powerful in Judah are stealing land and property from the vulnerable. He says these oppressors will ultimately be carried off into exile while their former victims redistribute the land among themselves. This improbable prophesy was fulfilled as the Assyrian invasion continued.

The annals of Sennacherib record that he conquered dozens of Judean cities and towns and deported their populations. This would have included most of the land-grabbers Micah describes here. But then, as other biblical accounts explain, because King Hezekiah turned sincerely to God for deliverance, as Sennacherib was besieging Jerusalem much of his army was wiped out by "the angel of the LORD." Some scholars believe this refers to a plague; whatever the explanation, Sennacherib was unable to continue the campaign and returned to Assyria. This oracle seems to indicate that the Judeans who'd been trapped in Jerusalem then redivided the vacant land by lot and fanned out to repopulate it.

⮑ Where in the world today are people being uprooted from their homes as land is stolen from the vulnerable? What can be done to oppose this? How would you respond to someone who said this was an inevitable consequence of progress and economic development, and while it's a hardship for some individuals, it's good for the society overall?

4 Have someone read the next oracle, beginning with "'Do not prophesy,' their prophets say" and ending with "that would be just the prophet for this people!"

This oracle describes how the professional prophets in Judah are trying to silence Micah. In their view, God is eternally patient and never carries out the kind of judgments Micah is predicting, so as far as they're concerned, his words aren't helping anyone. Micah responds by describing the extortion and oppression that are giving God good reason to lose his patience with the people and punish them with exile. He insists that his words "do good to the one whose ways are upright." But so-called prophets like these, who are happy to be paid in wine and beer, are in no position to appreciate this.

⮡ Does your view of God keep you from believing certain things about him, for example, that he would actively punish the wicked (or, for that matter, show mercy if that were appropriate)? Does this view make you selective in the teachings you listen to and the parts of the Bible you read and take to heart? Consider the view of God that admittedly has some biblical support but is most contrary to your own view and see what you can appreciate about it that will help you broaden your view of God and be open to more sources of potentially beneficial teaching. Group members can talk this one out together in your meeting.

5 Finally, have someone read the brief oracle of restoration that concludes this group, beginning with "I will surely gather all of you, Jacob" and ending with "Their King will pass through before them, the LORD at their head."

This promise of restoration could be envisioning the people's return from their eventual exile. (About 150 years after Micah, because of renewed apostasy, God allowed them to be conquered and deported by the Babylonians.) However, the reference to "the gate," a prominent image in the second oracle about the threat to Jerusalem, suggests that it may instead be describing the lifting of the Assyrian siege and the people dwelling safely in the land again. The idea of a "remnant" surviving and rebuilding the nation is a prominent theme in Micah's oracles of restoration.

⮡ Picture yourself as a Judean returning home to a rural town after sheltering in Jerusalem during the Assyrian invasion. What do you see along the way? What causes you grief, and what gives you hope? What do you think Micah meant when he said the LORD would go ahead of you? Returning to the present day, what's the closest thing to this you've ever experienced or heard about from someone you know? Share your observations with the group.

MICAH FORESEES A WORLDWIDE DELIVERANCE BEYOND THE EVENTS OF HIS DAY

Book of Micah > Second Group of Oracles

INTRODUCTION

The second group of oracles in the book of Micah continues the pattern of announcing judgment and then promising restoration. In this case, however, the judgment oracles are few and brief, while the vision of restoration is expansive. This puts Micah's best-known and most hopeful visions at the center of the whole book.

READING AND DISCUSSION

1 Have different people read the next three oracles, beginning at these places:

- "Then I said, 'Listen, you leaders of Jacob'"
- "This is what the LORD says: 'As for the prophets who lead my people astray'"
- "Hear this, you leaders of Jacob," (ending with "the temple hill a mound overgrown with thickets")

In these oracles Micah announces judgment against the various leaders who should be influencing the nation to follow the LORD, but who are oppressing and deceiving the people instead.

The first oracle targets the leaders and rulers who are responsible for establishing justice. Micah depicts them as wild animals tearing apart the people. They won't help the innocent Judeans who are crying out to them for justice, so when they cry to the LORD, he won't help them either.

The second oracle addresses Judah's prophets-for-hire. They, too, will receive no answer from God when they try urgently to hear from him as disaster strikes. Micah depicts them groping in darkness, and notes by contrast that he has been filled with power, justice, and might by the Spirit of the LORD. This is a statement of his prophetic calling, like the place where Amos says, "The LORD took me from tending the flock and said to me, 'Go, prophesy to my people Israel.'"

The third oracle targets the nation's leaders and prophets again, along with a third group, the priests, who are also exploiting the people. They all believe nothing will happen to them because the LORD is on their side. Instead, Micah insists, they're bringing destruction on the nation.

Micah's prediction that Jerusalem would be destroyed was eventually fulfilled, but not immediately. Perhaps because his similar prediction that Samaria would become "a heap of rubble" came true, the leaders in Jerusalem finally became concerned this would happen to their own city. The book of Jeremiah, written many years later, records how Micah's words swayed them: In response to this specific prophesy, King Hezekiah feared the LORD and sought his favor, so the LORD didn't bring about this disaster. Even though his mission was dangerous and unpopular, Micah ultimately influenced leaders at the highest level to change the course of the nation.

⮑ What kinds of leaders, in what fields, determine the direction of your society? Who, if anyone, is working to influence these leaders to follow God's ways? What impact are they having?

⮑ Hezekiah, as an absolute ruler, was able to change the character and course of his nation. To what extent does your country's highest leader determine its destiny, and to what extent is this leader's power and influence limited? Would you like to see this leader have greater power, to use potentially in godly ways, or less power, so there would be more control on his or her actions? Explain your answer.

2 Have people read the next two oracles, which turn to the theme of restoration, beginning at these places:

- "In the last days the mountain of the LORD's temple will be established"
- "'In that day,' declares the LORD, 'I will gather the lame,'" (ending with "kingship will come to Daughter Jerusalem")

This oracle about the mountain of the LORD's temple appears, in almost identical form, in the book of Isaiah. (Micah and Isaiah were contemporaries.) Scholars disagree about which prophet originally composed it and which one then repeated it; as we've seen, the prophets often allude to one another. (It's possible that both Micah and Isaiah made use of a preexisting composition.) This oracle depicts what will happen in "the last days" or "in later days," meaning "some time after this," possibly although not necessarily at the end of the world. It describes how, instead of being a place of injustice and bloodshed, Jerusalem will become a center of justice and peace that teaches the ways of God to the rest of the earth. The next oracle similarly depicts Jerusalem restored as a place of healing and comfort.

⮑ How do you envision these words being fulfilled? Do they refer symbolically to the effects of the proclamation about Jesus around the world? (See the next discussion point for how Jesus relates to the restoration oracles in this group.) Do they describe an actual period of universal peace and justice that will arrive within history? Do they depict conditions that will only be achieved through divine intervention at the end of history? Or might they be fulfilled in all three of these senses? Whichever view you take, what are the implications for your own present-day responsibilities? Whatever God is working towards, how can you work with him?

3 Have people read the next two oracles, beginning at these places:

- "Why do you now cry aloud—have you no king?"
- "Marshal your troops now, city of troops," (ending with "his greatness will reach to the ends of the earth")

While the previous two oracles were set "in later days," these next two address the situation "now," in Micah's own time, although they also look forward from there. Micah tells Jerusalem to be distressed, because its people are going to be carried off to Babylon. But this will actually happen in the future, once Babylon has displaced Assyria as the dominant power. So for the present, Jerusalem can take courage and stand up against its enemies, because God is going to deliver the city.

The means of this deliverance is explained in the next oracle. Micah promises a new ruler will arise in Judah. We have two clues about who this will be. He comes from **Bethlehem**, and his origins are "from ancient times." These things indicate that he's descended from the venerable royal line of David. Many scholars believe the oracle's initial reference is to the coming of Hezekiah. As we've just noted, he responded positively to Micah's message so that Judah was rescued from the Assyrian invasion. However, it's likely that this oracle, even though it speaks to the situation "now," also has a further fulfillment in the future.

Some prophecies, in addition to their original meanings, look ahead to a supreme deliverer God will send. This figure became known as the Messiah, the "anointed one"; prophecies that anticipate his coming and activity are known as Messianic prophecies. The book of Matthew in the New Testament identifies this oracle specifically as a prediction of the birth of Jesus in Bethlehem as the Messiah. As such, it looks beyond the current crisis of the Assyrian invasion to a divine deliverance with the same worldwide scope as the oracle about the mountain of the LORD's temple. Prophecies like this help us recognize that the restoration Micah envisions isn't just the return and resettlement of Judah's exiles, it's the transformation of people's relationships with one another and with God, through the work of the Messiah, all over the earth.

⮑ The prophetic portrait of Jesus as the Messiah has to be pieced together from scattered oracles spoken by different prophets at various places and times. No one who heard the words of only one prophet would get the full picture. Yet somehow those who collected and arranged Micah's oracles knew enough to put the one about a ruler coming from Bethlehem in the center of the book, together with the one about the mountain of the LORD. How do you think they recognized there was something special about this oracle that transcended its immediate reference to Micah's own time?

FOR FURTHER READING AND DISCUSSION

The remaining oracles in this second group expand on the vision of restoration.

- The one that begins "And he will be our peace" predicts the defeat of the Assyrians under the coming ruler described in the previous oracle. ("Seven . . . eight" is a Hebrew poetic device indicating a complete number; under this ruler, the nation will have enough commanders to meet the threat.)
- The oracle that begins "The remnant of Jacob will be in the midst of many peoples" describes how God's people will be a blessing ("like dew") to those who appreciate them but will bring judgment on those who oppose them.
- The last oracle in the group, which begins "'In that day,' declares the LORD," sounds like a judgment oracle, but it actually describes how the nation will be restored as God purifies it from militarism, occult practices, and idolatry.

GOD'S CASE AGAINST THE PEOPLE AND MICAH'S PLEA FOR THEIR RESTORATION

Book of Micah > Third Group of Oracles

INTRODUCTION

The third and last group of oracles in the book of Micah once again begins with judgment and then envisions restoration. In the judgment section, as also happens near the end of Hosea, God conducts a *rib* against the people, citing the history of their relationship as evidence that he's done right by them but they haven't done right by him. But then, in the restoration section, Micah pleads for the nation's rescue by appealing to God's merciful character and faithfulness to his covenant promises.

READING AND DISCUSSION

1 Have different people read the next three oracles in the book, beginning at these places:

- "Listen to what the LORD says: 'Stand up, plead my case'"
- "Listen! The LORD is calling to the city"
- "What misery is mine!" (ending with "I wait for God my Savior; my God will hear me")

In the first oracle, God rhetorically asks the ancient mountains and hills, as witnesses of the history of Israel, to hear his *rîb* (NIV "case," "accusation") against the wayward nation. God explains everything he did to lead them to safety in their new land: freeing them from slavery; giving them Moses, Aaron, and Miriam to guide them through the wilderness; defeating a Moabite plot; and parting the Jordan River so they could cross into the land (from Shittim to Gilgal). These actions at the beginning of Israel's history represent the centuries of care God has provided ever since. He has shouldered all of his responsibilities in the relationship; he's left none of them as a burden for the people to carry. But they have nevertheless abandoned his ways. Micah, speaking on behalf of the nation, asks what they must do to make things right. He describes various offerings of increasing value to establish that God isn't looking for some lavish payment to make satisfaction. Instead, God simply wants the people to return to his ways: to act justly, love mercy, and walk humbly with him.

Unfortunately, they're far from this. The second oracle continues the *rîb* by describing what the people have been doing instead of fulfilling their part of the relationship in this way. They've been cheating and deceiving one another (for example, with dishonest weights and measures, such as Amos described) and exploiting the weak through violence. Judah in the south has been just as wicked as the notorious King Ahab in the north. And so God's judgment will fall upon them. Micah announces a series of futility curses (for example, "You will plant but not harvest"), echoing, like Hosea, the end of Deuteronomy.

In the third oracle Micah laments that he can't find a single upright person in the land. He compares himself to someone looking for produce at harvest time but finding none. This image connects with the futility curses at the end of the second oracle, tying this lament into the *rîb* as a further indictment of the nation's violence and corruption. But at the end, Micah reasserts his hope and confidence that God will make things right.

⮌ Use the examples given here of God's early care for Israel as a model to help you reflect on what God has done for you. What specific acts of protection, provision, and guidance over the years can you cite as evidence that God has fulfilled the responsibilities of his relationship with you? Or do you feel that there are still some things God should have done for you that he hasn't yet? If so, talk this out with the group.

⮕ Micah says that God essentially wants us to do justice, love mercy, and walk humbly with him. What do each of these things mean? See if you can define them and illustrate what they should look like in your own life.

2 Have different people read through to the end of the book, beginning at these places:

- "Do not gloat over me, my enemy!"
- "The day for building your walls will come"
- "Shepherd your people with your staff, the flock of your inheritance"

While Judah experienced a reprieve under Hezekiah, eventually the nation returned to its corruption and oppression, so that in a later generation Jerusalem was conquered by the Babylonians and the people were taken into exile. Many interpreters believe that these restoration oracles at the end of the book were put together after the fall of Jerusalem from some of Micah's earlier sayings by Judeans who still remembered and treasured his words and believed in their promise—just as the song in the book of Amos may have been written by later followers who were inspired by his words. (Some interpreters argue that the oracles earlier in the book that mention Babylon and the exile are also later additions to Micah's original prophecies.) However, there's no reason why Micah himself could not have foreseen how Babylon, a threat to Assyria even in his day, would eventually become the dominant empire and how, unfortunately, the people would turn away from God once again and this time experience judgment at the hands of the Babylonians.

Whatever the source of these oracles, they end the book with a reprise of the hopeful themes that are sounded earlier. Judah or Jerusalem tells her enemy (a foreign country addressed metaphorically in feminine language) that God will now take his people's side in a *rîb*, pleading their case and winning their freedom. Then, as foreseen in the earlier oracle about the mountain of the LORD, people will come from all over the world to the restored Jerusalem. The final oracle in the book addresses God directly, pleading for his renewed care on the basis of his forgiving, gracious character and his faithfulness to the promises he made to Israel's ancestors.

⮑ The name Micah means "Who is like Yah[weh]?" The last oracle in the book asks, "Who is a God like you?" This may be a subtle allusion to Micah's name, acknowledging him as the source of the material in these final restoration oracles. Even more importantly, the question calls attention to Micah's appreciation for the unique character of God, which sustained him throughout his difficult mission. Reread the description of God that follows this question. List the characteristics it mentions. Is this how you usually think of God? Why or why not? Which characteristic means the most to you right now, in your own life and in your hopes for the world? Why?

To find out more about the spiritual struggles of the people of Judah at this time, and about their experience as exiles in Babylon, see the study guide to Isaiah in this series.

FOR YOUR NEXT MEETING

To prepare for session 16, group members should read the introduction to Zephaniah in *The Books of the Bible*.

ZEPHANIAH

EXPERIENCING ZEPHANIAH AS A WHOLE; ZEPHANIAH'S WARNING ABOUT THE DAY OF THE LORD

Book of Zephaniah > Overview
Book of Zephaniah > First Part

Before doing this session, give group members the chance to ask questions and share their reflections about the introduction to Zephaniah in The Books of the Bible.

INTRODUCTION

After Micah spoke to Judah and Jerusalem, three quarters of a century passed before another prophet arose whose words have been preserved for us. (See the chart on page 9.) Other prophets may have tried to call the people back to God during the reigns of Manasseh and Amon, but if they did, every trace of their messages was eliminated. Those kings were so committed to serving the Assyrians and worshipping their gods that any faithful prophets would have been killed or driven out of the country.

But conditions began to change towards the last quarter of the seventh century BC. Josiah, who had become king when he was only eight years old, was moving into adulthood and assuming the power to rule in his own right. He appears to have been guided in his childhood and youth by godly advisors, because when the occasion presented, he eliminated the idol worship that flourished under his father and grandfather.

Two things in particular provided this occasion:

- First, Zephaniah began to warn the people of Judah that they were facing severe judgment because they had abandoned the LORD. Josiah probably found Zephaniah's words particularly compelling because this prophet was of royal blood: Like the king himself, he was a descendant of Hezekiah, who had turned the nation back to the LORD in Micah's day. And so Josiah didn't oppose Zephaniah, but allowed his message to spread.[1]
- Second, the last great king of the Assyrians, Ashurbanipal, died in 626 BC. He had no strong successor, and this allowed countries like Judah to pursue more independent policies.
- With both the motive and the opportunity, Josiah purged the nation of pagan practices and called it back to the LORD.

In this session you'll read through the whole book of Zephaniah to appreciate his message and the influence it had. You'll also discuss the first part of the book. (The remaining two parts will be considered in the next session.)

READING

After a heading that identifies who Zephaniah was and when he prophesied, the book of Zephaniah has three main parts, beginning at these places:

1. "I will sweep away everything from the face of the earth": Zephaniah warns that the day of the LORD, a time of punishment, is imminent.
2. "Gather together, gather yourselves together, you shameful nation": Zephaniah announces God's judgment against Judah, the surrounding nations, and the city of Jerusalem.
3. "Then I will purify the lips of the peoples": Zephaniah foresees the restoration of Jerusalem.

Essentially the same phrase marks the end of the first and second parts of the book: "In the fire of his jealousy the whole earth will be consumed"; "The whole world will be consumed by the fire of my jealous anger." (In

---

1. The prophet Jeremiah began his own ministry around this same time. A guide to the book of Jeremiah is planned for later in this series.

Hebrew, the word order is identical and these phrases differ by only one letter, representing the difference between "his" and "my.")

Have three people each read one part of the book, beginning at the places indicated above. This should take less than ten minutes. Zephaniah comes right after Micah in *The Books of the Bible*; in most other editions, it's the third book after Micah.

As you listen, notice how Zephaniah echoes the words and images of earlier prophets. For example:

- He describes the day of the LORD with images of darkness, like Amos.
- He pronounces futility curses ("Though they build houses, they will not live in them; though they plant vineyards, they will not drink the wine") like Hosea and Micah.
- He warns the people, like Micah, that the LORD is not a do-nothing God (even though they're thinking, "The LORD will do nothing, either good or bad").
- He foresees the restoration of Jerusalem as a blessing to the whole world.

This illustrates how the prophets understood themselves to be speaking within an ongoing tradition, delivering one consistent message to Israel and Judah across the centuries.

DISCUSSION

Had you ever read the book of Zephaniah before? If not, but you'd heard of it, how did your experience of it compare with what you expected? Would you recommend it to someone who asked you to suggest a short book of the Bible they could profitably read and reflect on? Why or why not?

What struck you most as you listened to the book? What images or poetic lines were your favorites? Did any parts of the book trouble you? If so, which ones, and why?

⊃ Zephaniah's oracles portray the LORD both as a God of fierce judgment ("I will sweep away everything") and as a God of tender mercy ("in his love he will no longer rebuke you, but will rejoice over you with singing"). How can the same God display both of these attributes to such an extent?

Many interpreters believe that Zephaniah went to the Jerusalem temple during the Festival of Tabernacles to deliver his warning about the day of the LORD. They note that the phrase that's repeated at the opening of this warning, "I will sweep away" (*'aseph*), is a play on another biblical name for this event, the Festival of Ingathering (*'asiph*). These interpreters also note how Zephaniah refers to idolatrous priests and to superstitious practices associated with the temple such as not stepping on the threshold. Zephaniah also portrays the day of the LORD as a sacrifice, such as would have been offered in the temple, to which the LORD has invited guests—at which the disobedient people will be slaughtered ("Their blood will be poured out like dust and their entrails like dung"). If this understanding is correct, then Zephaniah chose a location and occasion that maximized the impact of his warning, but also the danger to himself.

With his call to "be silent," Zephaniah commands the attention of everyone gathered in the temple. He pronounces God's judgment against the foreign influences that are corrupting the nation. The continuing presence of idolatry, syncretism (worshipping both the LORD and Molek), and apostasy (abandoning God) suggest that Assyria remains a threat to be appeased—Ashurbanipal is likely still alive. Zephaniah is speaking perhaps a year or two before that emperor died, and he's making the subversive and dangerous assertion that the LORD is the true ruler of the world to whom all kings and peoples must answer. The biblical prophets are sometimes spoken of as if they looked off into the distant future and described things that had no real implications for their own day. But Zephaniah's experience, like that of his predecessors, shows that the message of the prophets arose from the real conditions of their own place and time and was often delivered at great risk.

⊃ Even though Zephaniah clearly understood that being a prophet meant being part of a great tradition, by his time no prophet in living memory had survived long enough to leave a legacy of oracles. What do you think it was like for him to accept the challenge of speaking to Judah and Jerusalem in his day? Do you think he discerned that the times were becoming more favorable? Or was he simply willing to accept death or exile if this was the cost of obeying God's call?

⮑ At the start of the next part of the book, Zephaniah holds out the possibility that the people could be "sheltered on the day of the LORD's anger" if they turn back to him. But in this opening warning, he simply announces that judgment is coming, and soon. Why do you think Zephaniah doesn't describe any opportunity to escape this judgment?

⮑ The people in Jerusalem thought, "The LORD will do nothing, either good or bad." How actively involved do you think God is in the affairs of the world? How about in your own life?

ZEPHANIAH'S ORACLES AGAINST THE NATIONS AND HIS VISION OF JERUSALEM RESTORED

INTRODUCTION

The second part of the book of Zephaniah is a series of oracles against the nations around Judah. Just like Amos's oracles against the nations around Israel, the series also targets the prophet's own country, in this case both at the beginning and the end. But in the third and last part of the book, Zephaniah, like the prophets before him, foresees Jerusalem restored as a blessing to the whole world.

READING AND DISCUSSION

1 Have different people read Zephaniah's oracles against the nations, beginning at these places:
- (Judah) "Gather together, gather yourselves together, you shameful nation"
- (The Philistines) "Gaza will be abandoned and Ashkelon left in ruins"
- (Moab and Ammon) "I have heard the insults of Moab and the taunts of the Ammonites"

- (Egypt/Ethiopia) "You Cushites, too, will be slain by my sword" (just this one sentence)
- (Assyria) "He will stretch out his hand against the north and destroy Assyria"
- (Jerusalem) "Woe to the city of oppressors, rebellious and defiled!"
- (Concluding general judgment) "I have destroyed nations; their strongholds are demolished" (ending with "The whole world will be consumed by the fire of my jealous anger")

Zephaniah addresses the foreign nations to the west, east, south, and north of Judah. (Like Micah, he makes word plays on some of their names. For example, Gaza sounds like the Hebrew word for "abandoned" and Ekron sounds like "uprooted.") The main offense of these nations is their *pride*. Judah's immediate neighbors have been encroaching on its territory, not respecting it as the "people of the LORD Almighty." The Assyrian empire is boasting, "I am the one! And there is none besides me." By claiming to be the only real power on earth, Assyria is asserting that it's beyond even God's restraint or control. (Nineveh has not yet been destroyed, so this oracle is being delivered some years before 612 BC.) One day, however, after God demonstrates his own power and reality, these "distant nations will bow down to him, all of them in their own lands."

The first and last oracles in this series show that the people of Judah and Jerusalem are equally guilty of *pride*. The same three groups of leaders that Micah described—officials/rulers, prophets, and priests—are acting as if they're above the safeguards meant to constrain people in their positions. (The priests, for example, are breaking the law instead of teaching it; the prophets are unprincipled.) Jerusalem obeys no one and accepts no correction. But Zephaniah hopes there are still some in Judah who will listen. Just as Amos called on the people to seek the LORD in the hopes of receiving mercy, and Micah urged his listeners to walk humbly with God, Zephaniah appeals to the "*humble* of the land" to seek the LORD, to seek righteousness and humility, and perhaps be preserved.

The series of oracles concludes with a verdict against the nations in which Zephaniah uses the same kind of legal terminology as earlier prophets. God says he will "stand up to testify," that is, give evidence in court. Beyond being a witness, he's also the judge: "I have decided," he says—literally, "This is my judgment." The judgment itself is expressed in terms reminiscent of Zephaniah's opening warning: When God says he will "assemble" the nations, this is the verb *'asaph* that's found in the name of the Festival of *Ingathering*, which can also mean "*sweep away*." And the last line of this oracle, as we've noted, is identical to the ending of the warning: "The whole world will be consumed by the fire of my jealous anger." Zephaniah wants his listeners to understand these oracles in light of the language and themes of the words they first heard from him.

⮑ Amos and Zephaniah speak at length to the surrounding nations. If the Bible is supposed to be the story of God's relationship with the people of Israel and Judah, why have these oracles been preserved within the Bible? What are we meant to learn from their admonitions and warnings?

⮑ Can you give an example of a government or religious leader who exceeded the rights and powers of their office through pride? What were the consequences? If a person made a deliberate commitment to respect the limitations of their position, do you think this would serve as an antidote to pride? In what other ways can a person intentionally cultivate the quality of humility ("seek humility")?

2 Have two people read the oracles in the last part of the book, beginning at these places:

- "Then I will purify the lips of the peoples"
- "Sing, Daughter Zion; shout aloud, Israel!"

Like Micah, Zephaniah envisions the restored Jerusalem becoming a center of worship for the whole world. God will "purify the lips of the peoples," including the people of Israel, so that in place of lying and deceit there will be genuine praise. Zephaniah depicts this praise in a marvelous way: Zion

(Jerusalem personified) sings for joy at her restoration, and the LORD is so delighted he sings along with her.

The book concludes with a final use of the significant language that was introduced in the opening warning. God says he will *remove* (sweep away, *'asaph*) the people who participated in the former idolatrous worship, but that he will *gather* the exiles and bring them home. *Gather* is a synonym for the other meaning of *'asaph*; earlier, Zephaniah said that God would *assemble* the nations (*'asaph*) and *gather* the kingdoms (using this same synonym). Zephaniah has delivered a consistent message, in consistent language: The unfaithful and disobedient will be swept away, but the humble will find mercy and be preserved.

⮑ If God "purified your lips," as described here, what difference do you think this would make in the way you talk and in the things you talk about?

⮑ Have you ever gotten the sense while you were worshipping that God was joining in with you—singing along, for example? If so, describe the experience for the group.

⮑ What's the most important thing you've learned or come to understand from your reading and discussion of the book of Zephaniah?

FOR YOUR NEXT MEETING

To prepare for session 18, group members should read the introduction to Nahum in *The Books of the Bible*.

NAHUM

EXPERIENCING THE BOOK OF NAHUM AS A WHOLE; NAHUM'S PORTRAIT OF THE LORD

Book of Nahum > Overview
Book of Nahum > Opening Psalm

Before doing this session, give group members the chance to ask questions and share their reflections about the introduction to Nahum in The Books of the Bible.

INTRODUCTION

Zephaniah, looking ahead a decade or more, anticipated the fall of the Assyrian empire and the destruction of its capital Nineveh. Another prophet, Nahum, spoke his oracles several years later, when the empire was in the midst of collapse and Nineveh was under siege. Very little is known about Nahum; the exact location within Judah of his hometown, Elkosh, can't even be identified. But it is clear that Nahum had a specific message from God for both Nineveh and Judah. The Assyrian capital, because of its corruption, greed, and wanton cruelty, would fall to its attackers, but the nation of Judah would experience renewed freedom and blessing as God showed it mercy and favor.

READING

Have people who are good at reading out loud and who are comfortable doing so take turns reading through the book of Nahum. This should take less than ten minutes. (Nahum comes right after Zephaniah in *The Books of the Bible*; in most other editions, it comes two books before Zephaniah.) A new reader should begin at each of the following places:

- The heading to the book
- Nahum's portrait of the LORD, beginning with "The LORD is a jealous and avenging God"
- Doom to Nineveh but comfort to Judah: "Whatever they plot against the LORD he will bring to an end"
- Nineveh will be conquered and plundered: "The shields of the soldiers are red; the warriors are clad in scarlet"
- Why the LORD is against Nineveh: "Where now is the lions' den . . . ?"
- Nineveh will fall just as Thebes did: "Are you better than Thebes, situated on the Nile, with water around her?"

DISCUSSION

⮌ While the book of Nahum contains a number of different oracles, they all have the same message: A great city will be overrun, pillaged, plundered, and devastated. Like the earlier prophets, Nahum describes atrocities being committed against women and children. How did it affect you to hear these oracles read aloud? What place does a book like this have within the Bible?

⮌ Are there people you know that you wouldn't want to read the book of Nahum? If so, why? Are there other people you would want to read the book? Again, if so, why?

⮌ Should followers of Jesus ever celebrate the downfall of individuals or nations? If not, why not? If so, could they use

the kind of language that Nahum does, including taunting
and blaming?

Nahum doesn't rejoice in the impending destruction of Nineveh out
of ethnic hatred—that is, he doesn't do this because he's a Judean and the
Assyrians have oppressed his country. Rather, he celebrates the Assyrian
capital's downfall as an expression of God's just rule over the whole world.
The first oracle in the book makes this clear. It's a psalm or song that praises
the righteous character of God and offers this as the grounds for everything
Nahum says God is going to do to Nineveh.

This psalm is written in a special form known as an *acrostic*. Its lines
begin with the successive letters of the Hebrew alphabet. Acrostics typically
have twenty-two lines, one for each Hebrew letter. Nahum's, by contrast,
uses only the eleven letters in the first half of the alphabet. (The psalm as a
whole still has thirteen lines because the thought introduced by the first letter
is expanded into three lines that all talk about "the LORD.") However, full
acrostics often have a break or transition in the middle, so that they're made
up of two distinct halves. Nahum may have composed a half-acrostic because
the halves of some acrostics could almost stand alone.

The poem begins by praising God's just rule over the nations. It then
describes his power by presenting a *theophany*, a picture of God coming into
the world with shattering effects, like the ones you've already seen in Amos
and Micah. Finally, it returns to describe God's character, this time contrast-
ing his mercy and care for those who trust him with his judgment against
those who oppose him.

⮑ The opening line of this psalm, "The LORD is a jealous and
avenging God; the LORD takes vengeance and is filled with wrath,"
seems to portray God as essentially angry and vengeful. However,
the term that's translated "avenge" and "vengeance" here is
almost never used in the First Testament to describe an individual
taking private revenge against someone they think has injured or
insulted them. Instead, it refers to communities or God defending
a victim of violence and injustice by taking action that punishes
the perpetrators and deters future aggression. If God does get

angry, in other words, it's when injustice and oppression need to be dealt with. This first idea in the acrostic may be expanded with the language about God being slow to anger precisely to avoid any misunderstanding about God's basic disposition towards us. If you've had the idea in the past that God is essentially angry (with you), does this explanation help you see God any differently?

⮑ Why do you think Nahum specifies that this God of justice is also a God of great power?

⮑ Where would you most like to see God's justice and power expressed in the world today?

⮑ As this half-acrostic nears its conclusion, Nahum mentions the name of the LORD again, but this time with a different emphasis. He says, "The LORD is good, a refuge in times of trouble." When you get into trouble in life, do you feel as if God is saying, "Serves you right, you dug the hole, don't expect me to pull you out of it"? Or do you see God as a refuge, comfort, and strength in difficult times? Why do you think you respond the way you do?

NAHUM DESCRIBES THE DESTRUCTION OF NINEVEH

INTRODUCTION

After the opening psalm that praises God's justice and power, the book of Nahum presents several oracles that all describe the destruction of the city of Nineveh. Through vivid imagery and intricate word play, Nahum uses poetry to narrate this event that marked the end of an epoch in the ancient world: Assyria's ruthless domination of the nations from Egypt to Mesopotamia was over.

READING AND DISCUSSION

1 The oracle that follows the opening psalm is connected to it by a shared phrase. The psalm concludes by saying that the LORD will "make an end" of Nineveh; this oracle begins by saying the LORD will "bring to an end" (the same verb in Hebrew) any plots against himself. The oracle alternately addresses "you, Nineveh" with warnings of destruction and "you, Judah" (or "Jacob") with promises of mercy and restoration. Have two people read the oracle, with one of them speaking the parts addressed to Nineveh and the other the parts addressed to Judah. (They should go through the oracle beforehand to identify their parts; in most Bibles, these will be separate paragraphs.

In some versions the names Nineveh and Judah do not appear in every paragraph; they're implied in the Hebrew and supplied by the NIV for clarity. The content will make clear at each point who is being addressed.) The oracle begins "Whatever they plot against the LORD he will bring to an end" and it ends "though destroyers have laid them waste and have ruined their vines."

⊃ This oracle describes how Assyrian oppression affected Judah: The people were strictly controlled (as if they were an animal wearing a yoke), they didn't have the freedom to worship their own God, and the fruits of their labor were taken away by their overlords. Prosperity and freedom will return when Assyria collapses. Where in the world today are people struggling against this kind of oppression? In the particular struggles you're aware of, whose side do you think God is on? What, if anything, do you think provides evidence of his activity to help this side prevail?

2 The next oracle in the book is a poetic description of the actual battle for Nineveh. A coalition of Babylonian, Medean, and Scythian troops attacked the city. Nahum first develops an extended image of bright colors and gleaming light to portray how formidable and swift these forces are. He then describes a natural disaster that helped doom Assyria's capital. According to ancient sources, just as these enemy troops were closing in on Nineveh, the river Husur, which ran through it, suddenly flooded and destroyed a strategic section of the city's vaunted wall, leaving it vulnerable to its attackers. Nahum depicts the defenders stumbling in their haste to reinforce the breach, and then he brilliantly uses the receding floodwaters as an image for these Assyrian troops fleeing to escape slaughter or capture. In another evocative image he compares the sound of women mourning over the city to the moaning of doves. In a word play that's difficult to reproduce in English, Nahum describes the city as "pillaged," "plundered," and "stripped": He starts with a short Hebrew word for the first term, adds one letter to make the second term, and then adds one more letter for the third, using lengthening sound to depict the spreading disaster. Have someone read this oracle for the group, beginning with "The shields of the soldiers are red" and ending with "Hearts melt, knees give way, bodies tremble, every face grows pale."

⮩ Do you think God caused the Husur River to flood in order to help the coalition that was attacking Nineveh?

⮩ Nahum describes the horrors of war in elegant, sophisticated poetry. What effect do you think this is intended to achieve? For example, is it meant to underscore the significance of the fall of Nineveh from the perspective of faith? Does it dignify the suffering of the victims of war? Or does this create a disconnect for you—should horrible events be described in language that's as shocking and disturbing as the events themselves?

3 The next oracle announces God's judgment against Nineveh. Nahum describes the city's crimes and then "the Lord Almighty"—God described by his military title, Yahweh of armies—declares that he is against the city and passes judgment on these crimes:

- Assyria is first depicted as a lion that ruthlessly tears apart its prey. "The sword will devour your young lions." God says in response, "I will leave you no prey on the earth."
- At the end of the oracle Assyria is called a prostitute and sorceress for the idolatrous worship it has imposed on subject nations and the wanton immorality that has accompanied this worship. God says he will expose this seductress as filthy and contemptible.

In between these two pronouncements of judgment, the oracle switches back to the battle that's carrying out God's sentence. Short, fast-paced lines of poetry illustrate the frantic struggle for the city.

Have someone read this oracle, beginning with "Where now is the lions' den . . . ?" and ending with "Who will mourn for her? Where can I find anyone to comfort you?"

⮩ In this oracle God tells Assyria, personified as a woman, that he's going to expose her nakedness and pelt her with filth (excrement). These words are spoken metaphorically, but they still raise the question of how God could tell anyone he was going to do that. What would you say to someone who asked you about this?

4 The book concludes with an oracle in which Nahum challenges the Assyrians to consider that if they could capture the supposedly impregnable city of Thebes in Egypt, then certainly Nineveh can also be captured. Thebes was built on a bend in the Nile river so that, as Nahum says, "The river was her defense, the waters her wall." But this didn't stop the Assyrians, who were able to conquer Egypt in two phases. The emperor Esarhaddon defeated lower Egypt (the northern portion, by the Nile delta) and captured its capital of Memphis in 675 BC. Then in 663 BC his successor Ashurbanipal went several hundred miles farther south into upper Egypt and besieged and conquered its capital, Thebes. In his annals Ashurbanipal doesn't explain exactly how he did this. He only states that he won a complete victory and carried away great plunder. The same fate is now in store for Nineveh: Nahum compares its treasures to ripe figs ready to "fall into the mouth of the eater." In the end the city's leaders will be killed and its defenders scattered, and "all who hear the news" will "clap their hands" for joy, because the Assyrians who have been so cruel are now being repaid in kind.

➲ Give yourself an important warning by completing this sentence: "If _____ could happen to _____, then it could happen to me, too."

➲ What's the most important insight you've gotten from the whole book of Nahum?

FOR YOUR NEXT MEETING

To prepare for session 20, group members should read the introduction to Habakkuk in *The Books of the Bible*.

HABAKKUK

EXPERIENCING THE BOOK OF HABAKKUK AS A WHOLE; HABAKKUK'S DIALOGUE WITH THE LORD

Book of Habakkuk > Overview
Book of Habakkuk > Opening Dialogue

Before doing this session, give group members the chance to ask questions and share their reflections about the introduction to Habakkuk in The Books of the Bible.

INTRODUCTION

It's likely that Habakkuk lived around the same time as Nahum, since he describes the Babylonians' rise to power. As is the case for many of the other prophets, we don't know much about Habakkuk personally. However, we do have one intriguing clue. The collection of his words ends with a musical composition whose style and instrumentation is specified, and which is designated "for the director of music" (presumably the one in the temple). This leads many scholars to believe that Habakkuk was among the Levites who were responsible for music in the temple. When Habakkuk speaks to God in the dialogue that opens the book, he uses the characteristic elements of a particular kind of psalm, as we'll see shortly. This, too, suggests that he had musical training and responsibilities.

Habakkuk is the only figure before the exile who's identified as a "prophet" in the heading to his collected works. (Amos, by constrast, is called "one of the shepherds of Tekoa"; the others are identified by their families and home towns.) According to the biblical book of Chronicles, some of the temple Levites had the specific task of "prophesying" to musical accompaniment, "using the harp in thanking and praising the LORD." So Habakkuk may have been a "prophet" in this sense, someone whose profession was to worship God in the hopes of hearing a word from God to share with the people. But in his case this definition overlaps with the other one we've been using to this point: A prophet is someone from any background who speaks truth to power. At this time when the Assyrian empire was collapsing, the people of Judah were looking forward to renewed political and religious freedom. But they still hadn't turned from their injustice and oppression. The word Habakkuk received from God was that as a consequence, they would experience another season of foreign domination. This word about justice and judgment was entrusted to a professional temple musician, showing that God could use insiders as well as outsiders to speak prophetically to his people.

READING

The book of Habakkuk begins with a dialogue between the prophet and God. Have someone introduce the dialogue by reading the heading to the book, and then have two other people take the different parts in this dialogue, beginning at the following places:

- Habakkuk: "How long, LORD, must I call for help, but you do not listen?"
- The LORD: "Look at the nations and watch—and be utterly amazed"
- Habakkuk: "LORD, are you not from everlasting?"
- The LORD: "Write down the revelation and make it plain on tablets" (ending, "he gathers to himself all the nations and takes captive all the peoples")

The LORD then pronounces five woes against the Babylonians. Have the same person who read the book's heading read the introduction to these woes

("Will not all of them taunt him . . ."), and then have other group members take turns reading them:

- "Woe to him who piles up stolen goods"
- "Woe to him who builds his house by unjust gain"
- "Woe to him who builds a city with bloodshed"
- "Woe to him who gives drink to his neighbors"
- "Of what value is an idol carved by a craftsman" (ending, "there is no breath in it")

Then have the person who read the introduction read the conclusion: "The LORD is in his holy temple; let all the earth be silent before him."

The last part of the book is a song that Habakkuk wrote, a prayer set to music. Have someone who has good dramatic expression read this for the group.

DISCUSSION

The other prophets you've considered speak declaratively from God to the people of Israel and Judah. Habakkuk begins by asking questions of God and he ends with a prayer. Should these things also be considered prophecy? Why or why not?

What contemporary musicians do you know whose songs you'd describe as prophetic in some sense? Explain why you chose them as examples.

A major theme of the book of Habakkuk is that those who believe in God need to be patient and trusting, remaining faithful while they wait for God to act. Why does God often appear to wait before punishing the wicked and rescuing the innocent? Is something accomplished through the delay?

Habakkuk speaks to God at the start of the book by using the elements of a particular musical form. The lament or psalm of supplication, which was developed more fully after the return from exile, typically began with a cry to God for help, which was expressed in urgent, emotional, and even accusatory tones. This was often followed by a description of the troubles the singer and others in the community were experiencing at the hands of wicked and violent people.[1]

Habakkuk's first complaint is that God is seemingly doing nothing about the continuing violence and injustice in Judah. Now that the Assyrian threat is receding, what can possibly motivate the people to change their ways? God replies that he's going to do something "that you would not believe": He's going to replace the Assyrian oppressors with the resurgent Babylonians, who will continue to chasten the disobedient people. In response, Habakkuk protests that this measure seems unworthy of a just God—it would be allowing the wicked to "swallow up those more righteous than themselves." The Judeans might be bad, but the Babylonians are *really* bad; Habakkuk describes their rapacious greed, luxurious self-indulgence, and flagrant idolatry. God answers that Babylon will ultimately be judged and destroyed for these things, just as Assyria was for its crimes.

This judgment is so certain that Habakkuk can write it on "tablets," large wooden placards that were the ancient equivalent of billboards—another means of wide communication in the biblical world. (The prophet Isaiah similarly used placards to proclaim his message.) God envisions heralds or messengers seeing what's written on the tablets and running off to spread the news of Babylon's inevitable fall. This won't happen right away, but it will surely happen in the future.

⟳ Do Habakkuk's impatient and accusatory questions (and the similar ones at the beginning of many psalms) suggest that God permits or even encourages us to talk like this to him?

⟳ If you could ask God any question you wanted, what would you ask? What do you think God would say in reply?

---

1. For more information about the different types of psalms and their characteristic elements, see the study guide to Psalms, Lamentations, and Song of Songs in this series.

⮑ Write up a dialogue between yourself and God that consists of an opening question and response, plus a follow-up question and response. Read it to your group at its next meeting or have two people perform it for your larger community in a worship gathering.

FOR YOUR NEXT MEETING

You'll be invited to sing or listen to Brian Doerksen's song "Remember Mercy" to conclude your next session. If you'd like to do this, find the words and music in advance, or search on the Internet for a recording or video you can listen to.

FIVE WOES AGAINST THE WICKED; HABAKKUK'S PRAYER

Book of Habakkuk > Woes
Book of Habakkuk > Prayer Song

INTRODUCTION

The LORD's second reply to Habakkuk flows into a series of five woes against the wicked. They begin as a taunt against Babylon spoken by the conquered peoples in response to that empire's downfall, but these woes then become a general condemnation of anyone—including any of Habakkuk's Judean compatriots—who's guilty of the same violence, exploitation, and idolatry as the Babylonians.

The book of Habakkuk concludes with a prayer that the prophet composed and set to music, asking God to renew in his own day the great deeds of deliverance known from Israel's past.

READING AND DISCUSSION

1 Have different people take turns reading through these five woes once more.

⮑ The first woe condemns people who "steal" from others in a particular way: They take advantage of the needy by forcing them into unfair borrowing arrangements and then seize the goods pledged as collateral when the loans can't be repaid. (NIV "extortion" is literally "goods taken in pledge.") Who in your society engages in predatory lending practices? What means do they use? Who are their victims? Have any of them experienced the kind of financial ruin that's ironically predicted here? If so, how did this happen? Do you know of any followers of Jesus who are working to make credit available to the poor on fair terms? If so, tell the group about them.

🔲 The second woe describes how people who profit from "unjust gain" build houses in what they believe are inaccessible places. What kinds of people in your culture live in homes that are inaccessible to the rest of the population? What are their homes like? Does the fact that someone has a home like this automatically mean that they're not living the way God wants them to?

🔲 The third woe condemns those who build cities and towns through bloodshed and injustice. Can you give examples of people who've done this in recent history? What means have followers of Jesus used to oppose them? Which means are the most legitimate and effective, in your view? Habakkuk says that violent self-aggrandizement is ultimately useless, because only God will be glorified in the end: "The earth will be filled with the knowledge of the glory of the LORD as the waters cover the sea." What do you think he means by this? What will the world be like when it happens?

🔲 The fourth woe describes how some get others drunk in order to exploit them sexually. What's the best way to warn individuals of this danger to them personally? Does this also happen on a societal scale—when getting drunk and high is glamorized through media and advertising, does this promote pornography and sexual exploitation?

⮑ The final woe is spoken against idol-worshippers who trust in objects that have no "breath" in them (or no "spirit"—another meaning of the Hebrew word). By contrast, the LORD is real and is "in his holy temple." Habakkuk is probably in the temple himself as he's carrying on this dialogue with the LORD. After hearing God pronounce these woes against the wicked, he tells everyone in the world to maintain a reverential silence out of respect for God's holiness. The idol-worshippers are calling to their gods without results; worshippers of the true God honor him by saying nothing. Have you ever found that silence was the most appropriate form for your prayers to take? If so, describe this experience for the group.

2 Habakkuk's prayer at the end of the book includes a lengthy *theophany* like the ones you've already seen in Amos, Micah, and Nahum. Habakkuk envisions God coming in power to scatter his enemies, who are represented by natural elements such as mountains and hills, rivers and the sea. While the vision is terrifying, it gives Habakkuk the confidence to wait patiently and trustingly for God to act, despite the difficulty of his present circumstances. Have someone read this prayer again for the group.

⮑ Habakkuk asks God to renew his ancient deeds "in our day, in our time." Would you like to see God do in your own place and time the same kinds of things that are reported in the Bible? Why or why not?

⮑ The theophany in Habakkuk's prayer may be a symbolic depiction of natural phenomena such as thunderstorms (lightning as God's "arrows") and volcanoes (mountains and hills crumble and collapse; Amos said similarly, "He touches the earth and it melts"). What natural phenomena speak to you about God? What have you learned from them?

⊃ In what situation in your life right now do you most need to wait patiently for God to act, and to trust him in the meantime? As a group, share with one another your thoughts about what can help a person wait patiently.

⊃ Did you like the way the book of Habakkuk included questions and a prayer in addition to its oracles? What do you think are some of the questions the other prophets (Amos, Hosea, etc.) had for God?

Questions about the pre-exilic minor prophets as a whole:

⊃ Was reading and discussing these prophets like what you expected it to be before you began this study guide? If not, what did you hear or learn or discover that was unexpected? Have you found that followers of Jesus today read and study the prophets as much as they do other parts of the Bible? If not, will your experience with this study guide encourage you to give more attention to the prophets, and to encourage others to do so as well?

⊃ How would you now explain what a prophet is? Are there still prophets in our world today, or were they only for ancient Israel and Judah? If you think they're still around today, name some people you'd say are prophets. If God had a prophetic message for you to deliver, what would it be? How would you try to communicate it most effectively?

⊃ If you wish, conclude by singing or listening to Brian Doerksen's song "Remember Mercy," which is based on the opening of Habakkuk's prayer.